C000010716

THE DALMATIAN

POPULAR DOGS' BREED SERIES

THE DALMATIAN

ELEANOR FRANKLING
M.A.(CANTAB.), L.R.C.P., M.R.C.S.

Revised by Betty Clay
and Marjorie Cooper

POPULAR DOGS
London   Melbourne   Auckland   Johannesburg

Popular Dogs Publishing Co. Ltd

An imprint of Century Hutchinson Ltd

Brookmount House, 62–65 Chandos Place,
Covent Garden, London WC2N 4NW

Century Hutchinson Australia (Pty) Ltd
PO Box 496, 16–22 Church Street, Hawthorn, Melbourne, Victoria 3122

Century Hutchinson New Zealand Limited
19 Archers Road, PO Box 40–086, Glenfield, Auckland 10

Century Hutchinson South Africa (Pty) Ltd
PO Box 337, Bergvlei 2012, South Africa

First published 1964
Revised editions 1969, 1971, 1974, 1975, 1987

Copyright © Eleanor Frankling 1964, 1969, 1971, 1974
Copyright © Estate of Eleanor Frankling 1975, 1987

Set in Garamond by BookEns, Saffron Walden, Essex

Printed and bound in Great Britain by Anchor Brendon Ltd, Tiptree Essex

All rights reserved

British Library Cataloguing in Publication Data

Frankling, Eleanor
  The dalmatian. — 6th ed. — (Popular Dogs' breed series).
  1. Dalmatian dogs
  I. Title   II. Clay, Betty   III. Cooper, Marjorie
  636.7'2   SF429.D3

ISBN   0 09 166580 9

Acknowledgements

It is with gratitude that I acknowledge the help of the following in the preparation of this book.

To the Kennel Club for access to some of its rare volumes and to Mr C. A. Binney for much helpful advice; to Mr R. H. Smythe, M.R.C.V.S., for so kindly making the anatomical drawings in the text; to Mr Gerald Massey for lending the illustrations of *Kitty Coaxer*, the Sartorius oil painting, and *The Duke of Devonshire and his Four-in-hand*, and to Mrs Bonney, the owner of these pictures, for permission to reproduce them; to Mrs Sanders-Watney for the delightful photograph of her tandem; to Miss Bourne (Thomas Fall) whose beautiful photographs, which, together with those of Mr C. M. Cooke, add so greatly to the value of this book; to the Dalmatian lovers in other countries who have kindly sent pictures of their dogs – Mrs Allman and Mrs Rhoda (U.S.A.), Frau Huch (Germany), Mr Colin Nelson and Mrs James Macdougal (Australia), Mr de Graaff (Holland), Mme Garaix (France), and Mrs Hammarlund (Sweden) – Dr Bernt (Munich) for permission to reproduce a detail of his photograph of *The Congress of Münster*; to Dr Richter, Director of the Dresden State Picture Gallery, for permission to reproduce *Hunting Dogs and their Attendants*; to English breeders who have supplied photographs; and finally to all the writers, past and present, whose work has contributed, directly or indirectly, to this book.

E. F.

Reviser's Note

TO THE FOURTH EDITION

The publishers have invited me to bring the fourth edition of Dr Frankling's book up to date as unfortunately the author's health does not permit her to do this herself. Virtually no revisions seem necessary to the text, but I have taken the opportunity of replacing a few of the photographs. I have also brought up to date all three appendices.

December 1973   I.B.C.

TO THE FIFTH EDITION

Dalmatian lovers throughout the world were grieved to learn of Eleanor Frankling's death in January 1975. The breed owes her a great debt, and we are fortunate that her love for and knowledge of the Dalmatian are crystallized in this book. For this edition I have updated the appendices again and added a new Appendix C on the Dalmatian overseas to augment Chapter 10. Three more photographs have been replaced.

July 1975   I.B.C.

TO THE SIXTH EDITION

To be invited to up-date Dr Eleanor Frankling's splendid book is not only a great honour but also a heavy responsibility. In the course of the twenty-three years since the first edition many changes have taken place and it has seemed right to record these while leaving the main substance of the text intact. I can only hope that the author would not be too disappointed with the result and that her book will continue to delight future generations of Dalmatian lovers. I acknowledge with gratitude the help given me in my research by Mrs Jean Rance and others.

M.J.C.

Contents

ILLUSTRATIONS

IN THE TEXT

Author's Introductions

TO THE FIRST EDITION

It has been a pleasure to write this book about the breed I love best. In the first two chapters I have tried to reconstruct the history of the Spotted Dog from the all too scanty material available. There is no doubt of the Dalmatian's antiquity and of its survival, unchanged in essentials throughout the centuries of its existence.

Dalmatians are now better known, more numerous, and more appreciated than ever before and the recovery of the breed during the past forty years, from the near extinction of the years following on the war of 1914–18, is truly remarkable. This progress still continues.

In the other chapters I have tried to be practical and useful, not only to breeders and exhibitors, but to pet owners, who need just as much help in the care and management of their dogs.

I have, for obvious reasons, omitted mention in the text of the prominent breeders and exhibitors of today. Their names will be found in Appendix C, which contains a list of post-war champions with their sires and dams, their owners and breeders, and their dates of birth.

Space limited the number of photographs; I should have liked to include more, for we have a considerable number of good dogs. I did not consider any dogs of which adequate photographs were not available; it is fair neither to dog nor owner.

Personal successes are forgotten in a generation but the names of famous dogs live on. It was so in the past, it will be so in the future. It is the breed that matters, and we, in each succeeding generation, are its custodians.

Bledlow, Bucks. 1964   E.F.

TO THE SECOND EDITION

I want to thank the many people, both here and abroad, who have been kind enough to write to me in appreciation of the first edition of this book.

I had hoped that the precise method of inheritance of deafness in Dalmatians could by now have been established but this is not yet the case. However, American scientists have discovered the cause of excess uric acid in some Dalmatians and details will be found later in this book.

Dalmatian registrations have increased at a great rate and many are not registered. This rapid increase can hold serious dangers for the breed which is emphatically not one suited to mass production (if indeed any breed is). Mass production is accompanied by mass export in many cases.

The breeders concerned have no knowledge of good breeding or rearing methods and their sole concern is profit. This is a revolting trade and little can be done about it. It is occurring in all breeds. I hope Dalmatian breeders will do all they can to maintain the standards of the good breed clubs in this respect, and be especially careful to whom they sell their puppies.

1969   E.F.

TO THE THIRD EDITION

In this third edition I have included the current breed standard in the text. A whole short chapter is now devoted to the uric acid problem and I have added a section on the round worm. The appendices have once again been brought up to date where necessary, and five photographs have been replaced.

Southgate, London, N.14. 1971   E.F.

1
The Spotted Dog
through the Centuries

The Dalmatian is an ancient breed and we do not know its original home. Unlike so many modern breeds it is in no way man-made. It has come down to us as a heritage from the past, an original breed with its elegant shape and spectacular markings, as curious and striking in their way as the stripes on the zebra.

Many and varied theories about the origin of Dalmatians have been put forward by writers of the past, but it will be seen in this chapter how little reliable evidence exists for any of them.

This dog may possibly have survived almost unchanged from the dawn of history. The late Mrs Hebe Bedwell owned a print showing clearly a dog of Dalmatian type, with excellent spotting, running alongside a war chariot, probably of Egyptian or Babylonian origin. We cannot be sure of this but it is possible that the eastern Mediterranean was the birthplace of the breed which later spread east to India and west over Europe.

Writers on dogs before the nineteenth century were few, and, at a time when books on dogs were lacking, communications difficult, and the knowledge of any individual therefore limited to the breeds he himself knew, those who did publish opinions must have relied on hearsay in describing many breeds. And so it happened that many alleged facts were merely pious opinions, put forward in good faith, but opinions for all that, and often second-hand ones. Moreover breeds as we know them today were very different. Pedigrees were uncertain, breeders used dogs of any breed which seemed likely to be able to add some needed quality to their stock, there were no such things as shows, and working ability was all that mattered. It is highly probable that even the most valued breeds have introductions of alien blood during a long lifetime, and no pedigree extended over a period of a century but would show one or more crosses, often with several breeds.

Nowadays we have a considerable literature on dogs and specialist books devoted to individual breeds, but one must remember that once a statement has appeared in print, especially, it would seem, in an ancient book, it is likely to be copied again and again without further verification until it is finally accepted as proved.

We must accept the fact that we know nothing with any certainty about Dalmatian origins. The name would suggest that the breed's birthplace was Dalmatia, now part of Jugoslavia. But the title Dalmatian seems to have appeared comparatively late in its history. For, as far as I can discover, it was first used in the *History of Quadrupeds* towards the end of the eighteenth century, with woodcuts by the famous Thomas Bewick, who supervised the text written by his partner R. Beilby. I have the second edition published in 1791 in which the section on the breed appears.

Spotted Dogs had been known long before this, here and in Europe, and Dutch painters seem to have included Dalmatians in many of their pictures.

We cannot, however, take it for granted that every dog with markings of black or liver on a white ground was a Dalmatian. There were hound breeds of rather similar markings which may or may not have been ancestors of our modern dogs, and the spotting of obvious Dalmatians of those days was nothing like as good as it now is. We can only judge by the paintings of the periods concerned just how like Dalmatians those breeds were. Many, I think, must have been the forbears of Spotted Dogs today. Readers will be able to judge for themselves from the illustrations.

Speaking broadly there seems little reason beyond its name to suggest that the eastern Adriatic coast was the cradle of our breed, and, as far as modern times go, the only Dalmatians known in Jugoslavia are those imported from England. Correspondence in the *Sunday Times* in May 1953 throws some light on this point. It arose from a letter headed

'Why Dalmatians?' which was answered by a number of people including Mr Vane Ivanovic of London who wrote:

'My stepfather, the late Mr Bozo Banac, introduced Dalmatian dogs from England in 1930. There was no trace of Dalmatians in Dalmatia before then. He bought the first two dogs and it was my duty thereafter to bring new specimens from England for breeding purposes.'

Independent and most interesting corroboration came subsequently in 1954 in a letter from Frau Brosius, then Fräulein Hüsmert, of Hagen, Westphalia. She wrote:

'Last September my parents and I spent a few weeks touring the coast of Jugoslavia. Though I knew that Dalmatian dogs are nearly unknown in Dalmatia, and in all probability this country is not their land of origin, I asked for Dalmatians everywhere, showing my photos. But no native had ever seen such a dog. Our last staying was the old town of Dubrovnik. Here I succeeded in finding people who knew a Dalmatian. They helped me to find the last Dalmatian in Dubrovnik. He was a lively, well-marked eight-year-old dog called Tommy, but very very shy. I had a long chat with the owner who told me a story perhaps of interest to you. But of course I can't judge what is true or invented. Tommy was said to be the last descendant of a stock of six or seven Dalmatians imported from England about 1930–1, by a wealthy shipowner, a millionaire. His name was Bozo Banac. The owner emigrated to America before the Second World War and died there. Besides, he had a kennel in the house he called Red House at Cavtat near Dubrovnik.'

Frau Brosius is a keen student of Dalmatian history, and one of the foremost German breeders.

It appears from the evidence in pictures of past centuries that Dalmatians belong to the hound group, and to that section of it which hunt by scent and not by sight. They resemble hounds to a great extent in conformation and their scenting powers and endurance bear out this view.

They are remembered here as the Carriage Dogs of the nineteenth century, but this function is comparatively modern and, as far as can be discovered, confined to England. In earlier times they were undoubtedly hunting dogs. Even today, with their good noses and staying power, they will hunt hare or fox if given a chance.

The earliest known picture which portrays animals which could easily be early forms of the Dalmatian breed is in Florence in the Capella della Spagnoli. It is a delightful primitive (*circa* 1360). One small lamb appears to be escaping, and the head of another is shown seized in a wolf's jaws. The spotted dogs are attacking the wolves with ferocity. This picture may well be the origin of the theory that the breed was named after the ecclesiastical white garment called a dalmatic, which with the black gown worn over it suggests the black and white of the breed.

On the whole, however, Dalmatians have not been well served by the early writers on dogs.

Writing in *British Dogs* (1903), edited by W. D. Drury, C. C. Lane, a prominent Dalmatian breeder of the day, ventures the opinion that the origin of the breed 'is not so obscure as that of many other breeds'. Few today would agree with him.

The first book on dogs printed in English was *The Boke of Saint Albans* (1480), said to have been written by Dame Juliana Berners, Prioress of Sopewell Nunnery. Nothing is said about a spotted dog in this book.

The celebrated sixteenth-century writers on dogs tell us nothing that can be thought to apply definitely to Dalmatians. These writers were Conrad Gesner, born in Zürich, author of *Historiae Animalium* (1587) in five volumes, Dr Caius, an Englishman (1510–1573), a 'doctor of Physick of Cambridge' and founder of the college which bears his name, wrote in 1560, at Gesner's request, a short treatise in Latin on English dogs, entitled *De Canis Britannicus Libellus*. This was later translated in 1576 by Abraham Fleming under the title *Of English Dogs*.

On the strength of this (reputedly not very accurate) translation, Fleming acquired a reputation for knowledge of the subject which it is thought he little deserved.

Gesner aimed at giving a comprehensive account of all that was then known about the animal kingdom. His work certainly formed the basis of almost all the Natural History up to the eighteenth century, and its author was described by the famous French Naturalist Francis Cuvier (1773–1838) many years later as a 'prodigy of learning, application, and sagacity'. Incorporated in Gesner's work, at his own request, was a description of British dogs by Caius. The only reference that might possibly be applied to the Dalmatian is the following sentence of Caius in a letter to Gesner: 'Recently (so fond as we all are now of novelties), a new variety has been imported from France, all white with black spots. This is called the Gallican.' In his translation of Caius, Fleming (according to Ash) added a statement which caused his readers to believe that Caius was referring to spaniels.

In 1607 Edward Topsell, a B.A. of Cambridge, published in two volumes *The Historie of Fourfooted Beastes*. The contents were, it is said, mainly copied from the works of Gesner, Caius, and Fleming. Dealing with hunting dogs Topsell writes: 'In Italy they make account of the spotted one, especially white and yellow for they are quicker nosed.'

Ash, commenting on this remark, writes: 'The reference to a spotted dog of Italy supports the results of investigations on other lines as to the origin of Dalmatians!' This is hardly perhaps a convincing argument.

Thirty years later Aldrovandi, an Italian naturalist, mentioned and illustrated a 'spotted dog trained to catch game'. This woodcut is reproduced by Ash (*Dogs, their History and Development* vol 2 page 6). The dog is hound-like in shape with black saddle and black patches at the roof of the tail and on neck and skull. The body, legs, and feet are covered with black flecks. The dog is rough-haired with a stump tail.

The seventeenth century produced paintings so closely resembling Dalmatians that there can be little doubt of the breed, though they are in no case named and the dogs are, on the whole, incidental to the main subject of the picture. In some cases the spotting is more like that of today than that seen in pictures nearer our own time.

Gerard ter Borch, the famous Dutch painter, depicted a scene from *The Congress of Münster*, 1647, preceding the Peace of Westphalia which ended the Thirty Years War. A detail which shows the Dauphin of France with his Dalmatian is reproduced here. There can be no doubt whatever of the breed of this dog.

Another well-known Dutch painter, Pieter Boel (1632–1674), included an undoubted Dalmatian with another dog, of Setter type, in a picture now the property of the Kennel Club, bequeathed by the late Martin Fisher, a prominent member of the Kennel Club and of the British Dalmatian Club. This Dalmatian has mixed black and brown colouring (the typical tricolour) and a blue eye. Its coat is long, it is dejected, and a poor specimen of the breed by today's standards. A really beautiful picture was painted by the celebrated Italian Francesco Castiglioni (died 1716) just before the close of the seventeenth century (probably about 1695). It is entitled *Hunting Dogs and their Attendants*. As the illustration shows, the scene is immensely vivid, the stags fleeing, the great negro, hawk on fist, and the dogs of Greyhound type as well as a Boarhound. The boy in charge of the two spotted dogs is typically Italian and the attitude of the Dalmatian across the sitting boy's lap is a typical Dalmatian attitude, seen often today, for many Dalmatians believe themselves to be lapdogs, and get as much of their anatomy as possible on to the knees of their friends. I believe that this attitude, quite apart from the dog's appearance, would convince any owner of a Dalmatian of their identity.

It is not until we come to the late eighteenth and early nineteenth century that we find illustrations and writings mentioning the breed by name and giving any information about it. Until then no known facts can be considered as proving anything but that there were spotted dogs of hound type in early times. The relationship these had to the Dalmatian of today can be a matter of speculation, though such a relationship appears to have existed. It does seem certain that the breed originated as a hound breed (braque) and it still possesses many hound characteristics. It seems also to have had a relationship to the old English Talbot, a hound which contributed, with the old Southern hound, to our present-day foxhounds.

A delightful Dalmatian portrait and, as far as I know, the

first painted by an Englishman, is attributed to the famous animal painter James Seymour (1702–1752). This undoubted Dalmatian stands against a background of green rolling hills on the edge of a cliff, also grassy. Its conformation is typical and its small spots are both liver and black.

This picture, and the famous Reinagle Dalmatian to be considered later in its chronological order, shows to a marked degree how little our breed has changed in fundamental type over the centuries.

We have so far escaped the exaggerations and distortions which show-ring fashions have dictated in some breeds. The priceless heritage must be preserved at all costs. Changes in type must be resisted, even if such resistance runs counter to the stream of contemporary opinion. Changes can creep in so subtly that the true conformation of the breed may be lost before the disaster becomes apparent. Some in fact may welcome such changes as 'bringing the breed up to date'. Such people should turn to other and less historic breeds, and not destroy a breed with centuries-old traditions.

An interesting picture by Christian Seibold, in the Dresden State Picture Gallery, shows Frederick the Great, King of Prussia (1712–1786), as a child of about six years old, an alert, half-smiling little boy, resplendent in Court dress, with a Dalmatian lying beside him, though all of it is not seen. A wary dark eye is keeping watch and the pose is one of alertness. Spotting is good, the rather dark ear, the only one showing in the picture, is marked with white.

In Berchtesgaden, on the borders of Bavaria and Austria, stands a beautiful old castle, belonging to the Wittelsbachs, the Bavarian Royal House. Although still partly lived in by its owners, it is also a museum and one room contains a magnificent cabinet, entirely made in an inlay of ebony and ivory. This was made by Heinrich Wahl, during the many years in which he was a political prisoner in Bavaria, and finished in 1750. The top section consists of an inlaid representation of the legend of St Hubert. This Saint, who died in A.D. 727, was the son of Bertrand, Duke of Aquitaine and cousin of the Frankish King Pippin. He was so fond of hunting that he neglected his religious duties. One day when out with his hounds and about to kill a stag, a shining cross appeared between its antlers. Hubert was so overcome with remorse that he fell on his knees and prayed for forgiveness. After this episode he completely changed his way of life, became a monk, and afterwards Bishop of Liège. Later he was canonized. The Belgian Canine organization, *La Société Royale St Hubert*, is named after him and the bloodhounds often used to be called St Huberts.

The panel shows the saint kneeling beside his grey horse in supplication. The stag stands a short distance away with a shining cross between its antlers, from which a shaft of light strikes St Hubert. The two hounds, surely Dalmatians, are close to the stag, one standing, its head turned towards Hubert, the other lying quietly nearby, both quite uninterested in their quarry.

Later, in the late eighteenth century, John Collet painted a delightful picture entitled *Kitty Coaxer Driving Lord Dupe towards Rotten Row*. It will be seen from the reproduction here that the Dalmatian has uncropped ears. I have a coloured mezzotint of this picture dated 1779, in which the ears are cut close to the head. The poodle in the small chariot clearly feels itself far superior to the Dalmatian, a coarse animal, which runs alongside.

In his comprehensive two-volume book, Edward C. Ash includes an illustration of a spotted dog by Riedal, and calls it 'English'. This dog has heavy Pointer-like ears and a heavy head. It is evenly marked with tiny spots, interrupted here and there with large irregular patches of solid colour.

Buffon the famous French naturalist published in 1790 a *Natural History*. This was translated into English by Barr. An undoubted Dalmatian figures in it with the caption 'The Harrier of Bengal'. This name appears here for the first time, without any particular reason that is known, and from then on this origin has been adopted by many people without further question. We shall see later how Colonel Smith perpetuated this idea.

Turning from paintings to another form of pictorial art, the woodcut, but still within the final few years of the eighteenth century, we come to that great artist in his own field, Thomas Bewick (1753–1828), and with him we begin to find pictures of Dalmatians, named as such and accompanied by descriptions, although brief and not always to be relied on.

Bewick's *History of Quadrupeds* was published at Newcastle-on-Tyne in 1791 and contains some of his famous wood-engravings, including Dalmatians. The main picture is accompanied by a paragraph on the breed; the second edition, which is in my possession, depicts a powerful, rather clumsily built dog, profusely spotted all over with very small spots. It has a patch over the right eye, the only side which can be seen, and its tail is carried almost vertically, with the tip curling over towards the back and is spotted closely on the first half. Its ears are cropped close to the head.

Bewick's description reads as follows:

'The Dalmatian, or coach dog has been erroneously called the Danish Dog, and, by Mr Buffon, the Harrier of Bengal; but for what reason it is difficult to ascertain, as its incapacity for scenting is sufficient to destroy all affinity to any dog employed in pursuit of the hare.

'It is very common in this country at present; and is frequently kept in genteel houses, as an elegant attendant on a carriage. We do not, however, admire the cruel practice of depriving the poor animal of its ears in order to increase its beauty; a practice so general that we do not remember to have seen one of these dogs unmutilated in this way.'

As already mentioned, I believe this to be the first time that the name Dalmatian has been given to the breed.

Apart from illustrations he gives in the *History of Quadrupeds*, Bewick added delightful little tail-pieces to his chapters, and two of these depict Dalmatians. The first shows a postilion-driven carriage of brougham-like type, drawn by two horses. It has the initials T.B. on the panel and Thomas Bewick himself is looking out of the window at the Dalmatian which gallops beside the carriage; a lively little work. The second, which figures in the chapter devoted to horses, shows a small boy cantering alkong on a pony with a Dalmatian running behind, followed by a manservant trotting soberly along on a big horse.

The letterpress of Bewick's book was written by his

partner R. Beilby 'being of a bookish and reading turn' as Bewick says. 'With this [the letterpress]', says Bewick, 'I had little more to do than furnishing him, in many conversations and memoranda, with what I know of animals, and blotting out in his manuscript what was not true.'

Bewick's letterpress may, as Vero Shaw later says, 'follow closely the dicta of former writers' and no doubt it does in the many other breeds and other domestic as well as wild animals depicted and described in this book. As far as I know, however, the author broke new ground in giving our Spotted Dog a name and a pictorial description. From then on during the nineteenth century almost every writer on dogs mentions the breed to some extent and illustrations are many.

It appears therefore that Bewick, or Beilby, is the first to impute lack of scenting power to the breed, one of the mis-statements that Bewick might well have 'blotted out'.

A number of other pictures are found in our own and Continental galleries which could be Dalmatians or could be other varieties of hound.

Turning now to the nineteenth century we find the breed constantly mentioned by the writers on dogs of the time. In many cases certain stereotyped remarks are made, such as that of Bewick, that the breed has no scenting power. Opinions were doubtless copied from one book to another, quite natural at a time when little literature on the subject existed and when many breeds must have been unfamiliar to those who had to write about them. The practice is not unknown today, and with less excuse. Opinions then had to be obtained from an informant who may himself have been equally ill-informed. One must remember that no dog shows existed in those days at which various breeds could be studied. Dalmatians also were then stable dogs, not the companions of their owners as so often today. They lived with horses and their owners saw them probably only when entering or leaving their coaches. Owners may well have known little of their capabilities other than staying power, and so little of their mental ability as to call them stupid, another legend still current like the first, and equally without foundation. As regards their reputation for stupidity, it is possible that this arose because of the defect of deafness which could well have been undetected in stable dogs and must have been far more prevalent then than in these days of control.

Hearsay is powerful, print is immensely more powerful. Even today a statement which has appeared in print is accepted as fact by many unsophisticated people, and so a body of inaccurate opinion is built up and becomes accepted, eventually becoming an unquestioned and unquestionable fact.

The nineteenth century opens with a book by W. Taplin, *The Sportsman's Cabinet* (1803). Little space is devoted to the Dalmatian, described as 'a breed of no value except to contribute to the splendour of the stable establishment'. But *The Coach Dog*, by Reinagle, of which a magnificent print appears in this book, more than makes up for the deficiencies in description.

The conformation of this dog is superb, it combines substance with good outline and elegance in the way a Dalmatian should, and its action as it bounds into the stable yard is full of life and vigour. Its blue eye and confused spotting are compensated fully by its beautifully muscled body and legs and its superb feet.

In 1837 a book appeared entitled *A History of British Quadrupeds* by Thomas Bell, a dental surgeon and teacher of zoology at King's College, London. The Dalmatian is mentioned as 'strong and beautiful but with little interesting to be said about it'. The breed is illustrated by a rather clumsy Dalmatian with a closed landaulette in the background after the manner of Thomas Bewick but without his skill.

In 1840 Volume Ten of *The Naturalists' Library* was published in Edinburgh entitled *Mammalia*. Colonel Hamilton Smith was responsible for it. He also adopted Buffon's Braque de Bengale theory of the origin of the breed, and one could easily assume from the text that he supposed this view to be original. His brief note on the breed is worth recording in full, since this view is widely quoted thereafter by writers on dogs, and emerges finally as a statement of fact, often quoted today as firmly established.

'From the general structure of the animal we are of the

opinion that it should be placed with the hounds; but though a very handsome species, inferior to none of the above in elegance of form and beautiful markings, it is, with some dissent however, said to be without power of nose or much sagacity and therefore invariably entrusted to the stables where it familiarizes with horses. Having, in the general description of dogs, noticed the print of a specimen brought from India with a white fur marked with small black spots, small half-dejected ears, and a greyhound-like form, we have thereby expressed the suspicion that our present coach dog may be derived from that individual of his breed, and we have accordingly given a representation of it.'

Colonel Smith gives two illustrations, partly coloured, the first of which he calls *Dalmatian or Coach Dog*. The dog is in profile, the spotting small and mathematically regular, resembling in distribution that of Bewick's dog. Colonel Smith's dog has a tan ear, continued on to the head as a patch and, like Bewick's, the feet are hare-like rather than the round cat feet we see in the Reinagle picture. The tail is carried in exactly the same 'pot-hook' manner as Bewick's Dalmatian and is regularly spotted over the proximal half in the same way.

The second illustration is labelled *The Parent of the Modern Coach Dog* and is exactly as Colonel Smith describes it.

We come next in our sequence of writers on dogs who have mentioned Dalmatians to William Youatt, a veterinary surgeon and a recognized authority of his day on horses and dogs.

His book *The Dog* (1854) devotes a short paragraph to the breed headed 'The Great Danish Dog' called also the Dalmatian or Spotted Dog. He writes:

'The difference between these two breeds consists principally in size, the Dalmatian being much smaller than the Danish. The body is generally white marked with small round black or reddish brown spots. The Dalmatian is said to be used in his native country for the chace [*sic*], to be easily broken and stanch to his work. He has never been thus employed in England but is clearly distinguished by his fondness for horses and as being a frequent attendent on the carriages of the wealthy. To that its office seems to be confined, for it rarely develops sufficient sense or sagacity to be useful in any of the ordinary offices of the dog.'

The breed is illustrated by Harvey who depicts a well-grown muscular dog of true Dalmatian type. Its spotting is profuse and blurred, with few white areas, its ears are cropped close.

And so, with little or no foundation, the prejudice against the Dalmatian builds up as regards its intelligence and working ability. The process is even too obvious, and still more obvious is the fact that so far none of these writers shows evidence of being familiar with the breed. The scissors-and-paste type of writing is not uncommon today.

The association or comparison of the Dalmatian with the Great Dane by Youatt in 1854, and repeated, as we shall see, by Stonehenge in 1876, did not originate with the former writer. As we have already seen, Bewick knew of this view but did not support it. In fact Linnaeus (1707–1781), the famous Swedish botanist and zoologist, included among the dogs mentioned in his works *Canis variegatis, or Little Danish Dog*. The association died hard for Youatt amplifies it in the Great Dane comparison and even Ash, writing in 1927, puts Dalmatians and Great Danes together in a single chapter, though of course no comparison between them is suggested.

The Great Dane of today as we know this beautiful and stately dog has long been known in Germany as the *Deutsche Dogge*. Apart from size, conformation of the two breeds is dissimilar in many respects, especially the shape of the head. Moreover the coat pattern in the Harlequin Dane is totally different from any type of Dalmatian spotting whether of yesterday or today.

We come next to an author who, with one or two others, was among the outstanding authorities on dogs during the latter half of the nineteenth century, at a time when a few books on canine matters were available. This was 'Stonehenge,' the pen name of J. H. Walsh, Editor of *The Field*. He was responsible for two books, the first *The Dog*, the first edition of which is dated 1867, published by Longmans, though the preface in my own copy is dated 1859. In this preface he acknowledges his debt to Youatt 'in the instances of some foreign dogs, both for the descriptions and also the engravings which are contained in it'. Stonehenge vouches for the correctness of most of Youatt's illustrations. His heading couples Dalmatian and Danish Dogs. His remarks in this edition are as follows:

'The Dalmatian is a handsome well-formed dog, standing about twenty-four or twenty-five inches high and resembling the Pointer in his shape, but usually having his ears cropped as shown in the engraving. He is beautifully spotted with black on a white ground, and being remarkably fond of horses and of roadwork with them, he has long been employed in this country to accompany our carriages as an ornamental appendage, but this fashion has of late subsided. Hence he is here commonly known as the Coach Dog, but in his native country is used as a Pointer in the field and is said to perform his duties well enough.

'The Danish Dog is smaller than the Dalmatian but being spotted in the same way, and characterized by the same fondness for horses, they are generally confounded under the term "Coach Dog".'

The statement on the relative sizes of these two breeds is probably the opposite of what Walsh meant to say but it was never corrected. Ash considers that his earlier work shows that he was not then accustomed to 'doggy matters' and relied greatly on what was told him. Stranger still that in the first edition of his next book Walsh made no mention of either breed though he had acted as judge at the Birmingham Show in 1860 (the first show of the type we know today with most breeds represented). He had withheld prizes from the Dalmatians.

Interestingly enough Walsh had included Dalmatians in a chapter headed 'Domesticated Dogs, hunting game by scent but not killing it'.

Walsh's second book was *Dogs of the British Islands*, published by *The Field*, of which at that time he was editor, and contributed to by various other canine authorities.

The first edition was published in 1867. The book ran through at least five editions and eventually included many highly controversial views on the subject of judging to a numerical standard of points, a problem now solved by the Kennel Club which has deleted the numerical standard of points from all its breed standards.

The second edition (1872) of *Dogs of the British Islands*, which, with the fifth, is in my possession, devotes a few lines to Dalmatians but gives no illustration. It includes the breed under the heading of 'Companionable Dogs', most of the names being now in the Non-Sporting group. This is a change of view from that expressed in *The Dog*, where, it will be remembered, Dalmatians were included, with gundogs, in breeds which hunt by scent.

By 1886 the book had reached its fifth edition and Walsh devoted over two pages of letterpress to the Dalmatian, giving a full-page illustration of Mr Fawdrey's famous dog Captain, to be mentioned later. He included a numerical standard of points and also a description in clauses of the points of Dalmatians. This constituted one of the precursors of the official standard which was formulated fourteen years later. It will be given with others in the chapter on the subject of standards.

Walsh begins his letterpress with the categorical statement: 'Without doubt the Dalmatian is a Pointer when at home' – he is careful not to state where that home is – 'but in this country he has never been used except to accompany a carriage in which capacity he is unrivalled.' Walsh appears to base this view on the fact that 'the English Pointer will follow a dogcart quite as closely [as a Dalmatian] though a Greyhound will not and will lag at least 100 yards behind'.

This time Walsh mentioned the Dalmatians he judged at Birmingham in 1860.

It is clear from the varying and even contradictory opinions of even one man at this time that the history of the breed was uncertain and confused, as indeed it still is, though only as to its origin. No longer do we wonder whether Dalmatians are like Pointers or Bull Terriers. We accept the fact that they are like Dalmatians, a historic breed centuries before Bull Terriers were made from the Bulldog and the old White English Terrier (now extinct)

with, Croxton Smith mentions, some Dalmatian blood to
give quality.

And now we come to another writer of the same period,
who wrote yet another book with the title *The Dog* but with a
subtitle. This writer was the Reverend Thomas Pearce,
using the pen-name of Idstone and the third edition of this
book was published in 1872. The Dalmatian or Spotted
Coach Dog, as Idstone calls him, has quite a good chapter to
himself, though with no illustrations; a pity, as the twelve
engravings in the book are delightful.

Reading through the various descriptions of the breed so
far, it becomes clear, as seems to be the case in any type of
writing, whether the author knows anything of the subject
of his own knowledge or whether his text depends on other
writers' work and his personal interest is small. There is an
inescapable difference between writing at first or at second
hand, the first is always livelier and more graphic than the
second. And now, for the first time, we find this graphic
writing in the work of Pearce. He clearly knew and liked
Dalmatians. He refers to Bewick's woodcut of about eighty
years before and 'the vignette of the docked Coach Horse
mounted by the old coachman who followed his young master
on a white pony: the same dog is drawn accompanying the
party, the object of the artist being to show the superior
beauty of the Shetland, undisfigured by shears, to the grand
coach horse and the handsome Coach Dog "improved"
by mutilation'.

The present-day legislation on docking and hogging of
horses and the cropping of dogs' ears would have rejoiced
the kind hearts of both Bewick and Pearce.

Idstone also has something to say on the then topical con-
troversy as to which other breeds our Spotted Dog most
resembles. He describes the Dalmatian as a Pointer with
Pointer instincts, having some Spanish Pointer blood. The
latter is the original of all Pointer breeds. It was a great deal
heavier and less elegant than the Pointer of today.

According to Idstone, a statement in *The Book of Prints*
(date unspecified), with which he disagreed, concluded that

'The Dalmatian should resemble the large-sized Bull Terrier as much as possible'. This appears to have been the prevailing view of a few years before.

Idstone mentions his inability to give the breed an origin and ends with a reference to Colonel Hamilton Smith's Harrier of Bengal, having included a number of anecdotes about the breed, and having greatly enjoyed seeing a Dalmatian as a clown at the Holborn Amphitheatre, in an act with a Red Setter and a Poodle. It is true that some Dalmatians are natural clowns and enjoy their acts as much as do their audiences, even in everyday life.

Next on the list of nineteenth-century writers on dogs, comes that great dog man of his day, Vero Shaw. His comprehensive *The Book of the Dog* (1882), in which he was assisted by the leading breeders of the day, was published in parts over a period of time and the only date in the two handsomely bound volumes in my possession is 1882, pencilled in with the name of the owner, Radcliffe Walters, and the inscription 'Bound in Parts'.

Vero Shaw's chapter on Dalmatians is fairly comprehensive. He mentions poor entries in breed classes at shows and remarks that few breeds attract more attention – but that the few good specimens seen at shows invariably attract surprise and admiration owing to the brilliance and regularity of their spotting. Shaw also is doubtful of the origin of the breed. It would seem that, as the years pass, writers got to know Dalmatians personally, to like them, and in describing them to rely on their own opinions and less on the statements of their predecessors.

Vero Shaw entirely disagrees with the view that the Spotted Dog lacks intelligence. Here we have, for the first time, a writer stating firmly his own opinions on Dalmatians: he writes: 'We can also render personal testimony to the general intelligence and docility of the Dalmatian.' He believes also that it has a natural aptitude to follow a carriage, and this, he believes, makes it unlikely that it is a form of Pointer.

Which of the two, Vero Shaw or Stonehenge, was the first

to make this point we shall never know; it seems more likely to be the former. A standard both descriptive and numerical is also given and will be considered later.

Mr Fawdrey's Captain is chosen to illustrate the breed, as he did in Stonehenge's book, probably the later of the two. It is a full-page colour print, which includes a Bull Terrier, the latter rather different from the Bull Terrier of today. This famous Captain had three names and three owners during the course of his career. Named first Traviser, and owned by Mr Lewis Boyce, he was sold to Mr Oldham of Manchester and re-named Uhlan, and finally Mr Fawdrey bought him and he became Captain. The two illustrations are unlike each other. Stonehenge's Captain has a good head with dark eyes, well-carried ears, superb spotting and a nice expression. The neck though short is nicely arched and the shoulders well-laid, the top-line level, the hocks well let down, the stifle well bent, and the legs well boned with good feet. Captain is extremely muscular and his barrel chest makes his body look heavy and clumsy. Vero Shaw's Captain has much larger and quite differently distributed spots, which are completely uniform in size throughout. His face and tail spotting is different from the Captain of Stonehenge and his muzzle considerably more snipey. The barrel chest is similar in both but Shaw's dog is higher on the leg and the colours show bright tan markings on the forelegs; in those days this was often considered to lend attraction to the appearance.

These are not photographs, one must remember, though plenty of faking can be achieved with those. They are paintings, and one is inclined to believe that the artists depicted this dog rather as his separate owners would have wished him to be than as he actually was. At any rate both paintings cannot be accurate representations of Traviser-Uhlan-Captain.

At this point in the history of the breed we must consider the Kennel Club, its position and purpose. It was founded in 1873 to bring order into the rapidly developing chaos of the increasing number of dog shows, held under no authority and with no common rules and regulations. Shows were gaining a reputation for malpractices of all kinds; there was no identification of the dogs shown, no system of registration, no authentic pedigrees, and dog shows were beginning to be regarded as disreputable affairs.

In 1903 the forerunner of our present system of registration was inaugurated by the Kennel Club. This was a system by which all dogs appearing at recognized shows had to be registered. This was followed in 1904 by a system of universal registration for all dogs covered by the activities of the Kennel Club and submitted to its authority. The result was the outlawry of those clubs and societies which had their own regulations. In spite of the outcry which can well be imagined, this action had the effect of raising within a short time the status of dog shows, dog breeders, and dog clubs.

Owing to the activities of the Kennel Club, this system has been the model for other Kennel Clubs all over the world. Details vary in different countries but the basic idea of registration is common to all.

Those who never stop nagging at the Kennel Club for what it does or fails to do might well consider the early history of dog shows in this country, and ask themselves what would have happened to the breeding and exhibiting of pedigree dogs, and what in fact could still happen, if no authoritative ruling body existed.

Our own Kennel Club is no more immune from human failings than any other body of human beings, but without it the dog game would have been impossible for decent people.

With the formation of the first Dalmatian Club in 1890 a new chapter in the history of our breed opened. Clubs to further the interests of several breeds had already been formed and there were quite enough Dalmatian enthusiasts to ensure a viable future for this old and well-known breed. Mr Droesse, whose name will appear in Chapter 3, was the first Secretary of the Dalmatian Club. He was succeeded by Mr W. B. Hermann who held office for many years. His wife was closely associated with him in the management of the club, and their daughter, Mrs Stacey, although no longer active in the breed, is still alive and a member of the British Dalmatian Club.

I am indebted to *The Dalmatian Handbook* (1957) by Mr Clifford Hubbard for information about the early days of this club, and Mr Droesse and the standard suggested by him for the new club will be mentioned in Chapter 3. Mrs Hebe Bedwell, then Mrs Hebe Wilson, whose Rugby prefix was famous for many years in the breed, was also a leading member. She died only recently at a great age. Other well-known names of this period and the first years of the twentieth century are Mr Newby-Wilson, Mr C. H. Lane, Mrs H. Carhew, Dr Wheeler O'Bryen, Mr J. H. Foster, and Mr Walker among others.

So far, as we have seen, and shall see in more detail later, every writer on Dalmatians gave his own idea of what a good specimen should look like. Some clearly knew Dalmatians, others both knew and liked them, others wrote from hearsay.

Now for the first time there exists a body to further the interests of the breed, to publish a true description of it, and to bring enthusiasts together into an organization to pursue these aims.

The first action for such a body is to formulate a standard for the breed, a description of the characteristics of an ideal Dalmatian.

The standard of the new club is especially important because it is the basis of all other existing Dalmatian standards throughout the world.

And so, with the approach of the new century, our breed emerges into a new era of development and advance, with the mystery of its birth still unsolved but with England as its cradle and its nursery. We can congratulate the compilers of this new standard, which will be considered in detail in the chapter devoted to standards. While describing the points of a good Dalmatian, it insists on 'moderation' and thus avoids the tendency to exaggerations. It is largely owing to this insistence that our present-day Dalmatians are still, in essentials, what they have been throughout their long and

honourable history. It is the responsibility of every succeeding generation that they should so remain.

In 1903 the North of England Dalmatian Club was born,
to cater for growing interest in the north, chiefly in the
Manchester area. The new club adopted the standard of
1890 in its entirety except for the weight of bitches. Its
founder members included Dr Armistead (President), Mr R.
D. Blackburn (Honorary Secretary and Treasurer), Mr J.
Broughton, Mr J. Hodgkinson, Mr Howarth, all committee
members. Other early and well-known members were
Mr William Proctor, Mr A. R. Fish, Mr G. A. Bury, and his
brother Mr C. Bury, Mr W. Whittaker, and Mr J. C.
Preston.

An important event early in the new century was the
founding of the Dalmatian Club of America. This club with
its history will be mentioned in Chapter 9.

Records during the first twenty-five years of this century
are few. As the motor car gradually replaced the carriage and
pair, the dog cart, and phaeton, Dalmatians seemed to some
people to have lost the reason for their existence. However,
C. H. Lane, a well-known Dalmatian breeder and exhibitor,
devoted eight pages to the breed in his article in the
excellent two-volume book on dogs edited by W. D. Drury,
entitled *British Dogs*.

In the third edition (1903) he emphasizes Dalmatian
qualities as a carriage dog, as indeed it still was, though its
day in this capacity was nearly over. He mentions anecdotes
about the breed, and disposes of the idea that following
carriages was its only occupation. In fact Lane clearly loved
Dalmatians and the list of his winners is impressive. Two
photographs are included in his article, those of Mr Newby-
Wilson's black-spotted Ch. Moujik and Dr Wheeler O'Bryen's
liver Melton. If these are accurate representations of the
dogs neither would be among the top winners of today.

I know of no records of the breed during the second
decade of the century apart from the invaluable records of
the Kennel Club Stud Books giving particulars of the top
winning dogs with pedigrees and awards.

A period during which written information is lacking in breed history becomes a new sort of Dark Ages for those who come after and have themselves no memory of the period. And so from about 1910 for about fifteen years or more we have little information to help us.

The First World War was a time of great difficulty, especially when food rationing was imminent in 1916. Pressure from government circles for the destruction of dogs was countered by the Kennel Club, then as now anxious to do all that could be done for their welfare, by an offer to cease general registrations until such time as the emergency was over. This offer was accepted and resulted in a gap in the pedigrees of offspring of many dogs between 1917 and 1920.

Far back in the pedigree of today's Dalmatians names of dogs of pedigree unknown will be found. At that time and for years afterwards these names will have been known to the breeders and others, though officially they remained unknown, but with their death and the eventual disappearance from the scene of their owners, this knowledge has been lost.

How fortunate we are today with our records. These cover the period from 1934 to the present day, in the British Dalmatian Club's Handbooks, published annually from 1934 to 1938 inclusive, and after the 1939–45 War, beginning in 1949, at roughly three-yearly intervals, each covering the entire period in its records since the preceding edition. Future historians of the Dalmatian will look on these books as beyond price, as indeed they are.

In order to fill in some gaps in the breed history for those who have joined more recently, the BDC commissioned reprints of the Club Handbooks for the years 1934, 1935 and 1936, complete with photographs. These were limited editions and are full of interest to all who were fortunate enough to obtain a copy.

Fortunately indeed for this ancient breed of Dalmatians the Dark Ages of the earlier part of the century were succeeded, as were the Dark Ages of History, by a splendid Renaissance.

2

The Dalmatian of Today

The end of the 1914–18 War and the years immediately following saw a breed sadly depleted, not only by the stringencies of the time but by the interruption of registrations, possibly also by the muzzling order imposed on all dogs owing to rabies brought in by dogs from abroad. This lasted until 1922.

Only two Dalmatians were registered when this again became possible. Naturally a number of unregistered animals were in existence and the names of these are to be found in extended pedigrees of all our dogs today. Their breeding was not unknown then, but with the lapse of time and the absence of all printed records they themselves are hardly remembered and their parents are unknown.

The first champion to gain her title after the war was Mrs Bedwell's Rugby Beauty's Eyes in 1922, recorded by James Saunders in his little book *The Dalmatian and All About It*, long since out of print.

In 1921 three other animals became champions, Ch. Panworth, born in 1914, owned by the late Mr Kemp, Ch. Penwortham Major born 1920, owned by Mr Fish, and Ch. Gran Spumante, a bitch, born also in 1920, owned by Mr G. A. Bury.

In his foreword to the first handbook of what is now the British Dalmatian Club, not then in existence, Mr Will Hally, that great canine authority, wrote:

'If any of you younger fanciers want to know from what almost negligible numbers of post-war Dalmatian fancy was developed, ask Mr Kemp to tell you of the Kennel Club Show at the Crystal Palace in 1920. There was one Dalmatian, one Dalmatian exhibitor, and two Dalmatian enthusiasts. Mr Kemp was the exhibitor, Champion Panworth (not then

35

a champion) was the exhibit, and he and I were the optimists. Everybody else was telling everybody else that the Dalmatian was the last survivor, a relic of a breed that had gone, and a whole lot of other commiserating comments. There were sneers and laughter too, for who would bother about a breed that was all "past" and no "future". I think Mr Kemp's determination was born again that day, just as I went home feeling that the last laugh would be mine.'

Interest in Dalmatians grew gradually in the south, though the original Dalmatian Club was beginning to lose ground.

The next step had far-reaching results for the breed. In 1925 a meeting was held at Crufts (then at the old Agricultural Hall in Islington), owing to the enthusiasm of seven exhibitors and in order to stimulate interest in Dalmatians in southern England. A new Dalmatian Club was conceived there and was born during that year, with Mr Kemp as its first President, Mrs Kemp as its Honorary Secretary-Treasurer, and Mrs Mackie as its Chairman. It was named the Southern Dalmatian Club.

Its handful of members increased, first slowly, then more rapidly. By the beginning of 1926 the membership was 34. By the time I became a member in 1927 I believe the number had grown to about 60. The new club expanded its boundaries very soon after its birth.

Nineteen-thirty was an eventful year in the history of the Southern Dalmatian Club, for it saw the first specialist show in the breed, a limited event. It was held at Tattersalls in Knightsbridge, a most suitable spot for Dalmatians. The old building is now demolished but will remain a nostalgic memory as long as exhibitors of those days survive.

This show was a spectacular success with a record entry of 458 which is still unbeaten. We who were there will never forget it. It was judged by the late Mr W. J. Nichols and by Mr James Saunders.

In the same year the North of England Dalmatian Club held its own first show, an open event at Bolton, judged by the late Mr Geoffrey Gush and the late Mr Fred Wardell. Mr

Gush was by this time Chairman of the South of England Club owing to the death of Mrs Mackie.

Also in 1930 another important event in Dalmatian history occurred. This was the change of name of the South of England Dalmatian Club to that of the British Dalmatian Club. The reason for the change was the rapid growth in membership and its spread throughout the country. With boundaries and influence so widely expanded, it had become clear that the new club was national rather than local.

In 1933 the British Dalmatian Club gained championship status for its show, again held in April which has been the traditional month ever since and the show has been held in sequence unbroken except for the war years, 1940–5, although in the latter year, owing to post-war circumstances, it had to be an open show. From 1946 onwards there have been no interruptions in the sequence.

The All-Ireland Dalmatian Club was founded in 1934 by a handful of enthusiasts. Its first President was Mrs J. Mackay and its Hon. Secretary and Treasurer was Miss D. Gaisford St Lawrence who retained this office until 1965. The club owes a great deal to her devotion in keeping things going through the difficult war years and immediately after.

Other notable supporters have been the late Air Commodore and Mrs Gore (Duxfordham) and the late Mrs Wigglesworth (Goworth). The present Hon. Sec. and Treasurer is Mr J. P. Cunningham. Mrs E. Simonds is President and Miss Oonah Gore Vice-President.

Breeders and exhibitors of today, who have profited by the struggle of Dalmatian lovers of those early days, dedicated to the breed and determined to save it from oblivion, might sometimes remind themselves of the debt they owe. Their path has been made smooth by the efforts of others, whose mainspring was not the desire for personal fame but an unswerving love for a fine historical breed and the resolve to preserve it.

Looking back to the twenties and thirties, it is naturally not possible to mention the name of every well-known breeder and exhibitor of that period. A number, however, must be recorded for their dogs were, in the main, among the best of their day and are part of the history of the breed. These names and their famous prefixes will never be forgotten.

Mr and Mrs Kemp (Coldharbour), Mrs Bedwell (Rugby), Miss Parson, Mr Proctor, Mr Fish (Penwortham), Mrs Wigglesworth (Goworth), Dr and Mrs Hackney, Major Pirie, Miss Evelyn Barnes (of the Wells), Miss Veasey (Hyders), Mr J. B. Newman (of the Highway), Miss Shirley Mallion (Silverden), Mrs Gatheral (Phaeland), Miss Clay (Tantivvey), Miss Monkhouse (Cabaret), Mr Willie Greenwood (Tandem), Mr Gush (Roadcoach), Mr Frank and Mr Fred Makin, Mrs Bloomfield (Welfield), Miss Millie Stephens (Coelan), Miss B. Stevens (Gambia), Captain, now Sir Ambrose, Keevil (Caefel), Mrs Bland (Four-in-Hand), Mrs and Miss Beal (Stubbington), Mrs Leighton Yeomans (Astwood), Mrs Eggo (Mesra), Mrs Gore (then Duxford, now Duxfordham), Mr Emerson (Orchid), Mrs Nixey (of Birch), Miss Smither (Aldham), Lieut.-Commander Hamilton (Dibden), Miss Grant-Ives (Standsure), Mrs Ratcliffe (Littleknowle), Miss Paterson (of Brow), Miss Macfie (Colonsay), Mrs J. Williams (Modsley), Mr and Mrs Byrd (Spurstow), Mrs Walford (Midstone), Mrs Moseley (Highwood), Mrs Curphey (Muggins), Mrs Walker-Smith (Bookham).

Among the best known Dalmatians of the period were Ch. Snow Leopard, Ch. the Warrior of Hyders, Ch. Lucky James, Ch. Bookham Swell, Ch. Group Captain of the Highway, Ch. Coelan Leader, Ch. Goworth Victor, Ch. Cabaret Crofty Cock, Ch. Mesra Madeleine, Ch. Orchid Colmartin, Ch. Buckshot, Ch. Lead of Trumps, Ch. Venus of the Wells, Ch. Gwen of the Wells, Ch. Ace of Tricks, Ch. Poetebcross Prince, Ch. Mistress Quickly, Ch. Ervilliers of Spurstow, Ch. George of the River, Ch. Poulton Faloudah, Ch. Happy Sally, Ch. Cabaret Copyright, Ch. Hannah of the Highway, Ch. Moonmagic of Chasefield, Ch. Aldham Susannah, Ch. Phyrefly of the Phorest. George of the River distinguished himself by siring four champions out of Miss Clay's Patrician Maid, three English and one American.

Bringing the record of British Clubs up to date, in March 1970 the Dalmatian Club of Scotland was formed, to cater for enthusiasts over the Border. The first President was Mr I. B. T. Simpson; Mr J. S. Hally, Chairman, and Mr A. C. Taaffe, Secretary. The Club held its first Open show in September of the same year and first championship show in 1973. Both of these highly successful events are now held annually. The present club officials are: Mrs A. Simpson (President), Mr G. McVicar (Chairman), and Mrs C. Whyte (Secretary).

Dalmatians of Today
Champions from 1964 will be found towards the end of Appendix C. Our Dalmatians today compare quite favourably with those of the past, perhaps because we have so many more of them and therefore more chances of first-class breeding stock.

We have not yet eliminated all faults of conformation, of which, in the writer's opinion, the worst are bad hind action in many and rather coarse heads in a few.

We rarely see cow hocks or bowed legs in the Dalmatian today, but too often the hind feet in action are too close together, they do not move directly behind the forelegs as they should – the forelegs should be invisible from behind. Under-developed muscles, caused by lack of exercise, could be the reason for this fault, which usually includes flat quarters, lack of development of the thigh muscles and those of the second thigh, which is too often seen in the show-ring in otherwise good dogs.

The correct Dalmatian head has a long and powerful muzzle.

Happily we see fewer upright shoulders and straight stifles, shallow briskets and flat ribs than formerly. In general decoration is excellent; one sees only the very occasional curled tail and a nervous or bad-tempered animal is exceedingly rare.

We are fortunately free from most of the hereditary defects of today. They must have been in existence for many years without being recognised as hereditary. Hip dysplasia was probably dismissed as just lameness, entropion as inflamed eyes. Deafness is still with us and will be dealt with in another chapter.

Registrations have steadily increased, from 1658 in 1964 to 2916 in 1969. This rapid increase in numbers is not an unqualified benefit to the breed, for commercialism creeps in when popularity opens the door.

A number of new breeders, members of neither club, are breeding Dalmatians solely for profit. Neither the Kennel Club nor the breed clubs have any jurisdiction over this practice, for many puppies are not registered. They are often badly reared and undersized, and are sold at high prices, often for mass export. It is tragic that a truly historic breed should be the victim of purely commercial interest, with no concern for the welfare of the individual or the breed itself.

The status of the Dalmatian, nevertheless, is steadily improving, mainly because the breed clubs are determined to safeguard its future. Dalmatians are now among the breeds to be reckoned with for the top awards in the big ring at every championship show.

The highlight of 1968 was the award of Best in Show All Breeds at Crufts to Mrs Woodyatt's lovely bitch, Ch. Fanhill Faune, winner of twenty challenge certificates. She was difficult to fault, either in appearance or in the wonderful temperament she inherited from her famous dam, Ch. Fanhill Fleur of Queenwood, also bred by Mrs Woodyatt.

Dalmatians are not included in the working or sporting breeds in England. In Holland they are in the sporting group. They are extremely intelligent and quick to learn and are capable of a variety of types of work. They could almost be called Jacks of All Trades. They are easily trained by gentle methods and harsh or rough methods are quite out of place in this breed. They can make good gundogs: the writer sold two, both of which were successful. One bitch took it in her stride to swim across a river to pick up a wounded bird and swim back to deliver it to hand in the approved manner. The Dalmatian is good at Obedience and really enjoys it; one or two have made good Guide Dogs for the Blind; as companions they could not be better, for they are affectionate, obedient (when trained) and as house dogs they are discriminating and safe.

In the meantime the affairs of the British Dalmatian Club were managed with great efficiency. On Mrs Mackie's retirement as Chairman in 1928, Mr Geoffrey Gush of the Roadcoach prefix was elected Chairman and retained this office until his death soon after the end of the 1939–45 War, with the exception of a single year when Miss Evelyn Barnes held office. Mrs Kemp resigned as Secretary in 1931 and was succeeded by Mr W. E. C. Greenwood who remained in charge for several years. After a short interval, during which another secretary was appointed, Mr Charles Clover took over and worked hard and long in the interest of the club. He died after a long illness in November 1963.

How then did the Dalmatians of this period compare with those of today? My opinion is that while the best animals of the thirties were as good as those of the present, the general average nowadays is higher.

The war was a great set-back to all breeds. The last championship show for eight years was held at Harrogate on its very eve. Not unnaturally there were many absentees. For a time open and sanction shows were permitted by the Kennel Club, though the number was greatly reduced. But in 1942, with all the trouble and difficulties of the time, the Kennel Club wisely decided that only 'Radius' shows could be allowed. Entries for these were restricted to dogs living within twenty-five miles of the venue. These shows were considered by the authorities to be, and actually were, a useful form of relaxation for the countless people who by then were engaged in work of national importance of all kinds. They served their purpose, but from the point of view of many of the less numerically strong breeds they were of little or no use in maintaining standards. Dogs could do an immense amount of winning without having met more than one or two, possibly even none, of their own breed. In this way many owners who came into the breed during the war got an entirely fictitious idea of their dogs' merits. In addition most pre-war enthusiasts were engaged in war efforts which put a stop to their doggy activities and only the lucky few were able to keep a nucleus of their kennels in being for a future revival should the war end in victory for the Allies, and this was by no means certain during the earlier years of hostilities.

Fortunately, though little breeding took place during the war, a nucleus of good dogs survived to start the breed again, though, with some notable exceptions, it had deteriorated sadly in type and soundness. In a way we had to make a new start, though from a much higher level both in numbers and merit than that from which we started after the First World War just over twenty-five years before.

Both clubs were naturally dormant during the major part of the war, though the British Club held an open show in London in April 1940 shortly before the German attack on Holland and Belgium. After this the war started in earnest.

With the return of peace in 1945 the clubs went into action. Mr Clover remained the Secretary of the British Club, while Mr Lewis took over the post for the North of England Club, and Mrs W. B. Hermann that of the old Dalmatian Club. The latter, however, had lost its momentum during its long life; its members were few and mostly inactive. It lingered on in a state of suspended animation until 1947 when it officially expired.

The first post-war Dalmatian Show was held by the British Dalmatian Club on 3 October 1945, at the London Scottish Drill Hall, and the first Annual General Meeting for five and a half years was held at this show. Mrs Nixey was elected the new Chairman and the late Mr Martin Fisher was elected Vice-Chairman in his absence, as he was still serving in India.

This was an open unbenched show, for benching was the great problem of the show world, and it remained so for some time. There was an excellent entry of 263 at this show. The late Mrs Wigglesworth judged dogs, the late Miss Barnes bitches. Classes were crowded, for every exhibit, with the exception of age-restricted classes (puppies, juniors, and veterans) or pre-war winning dogs, were eligible for every class, for obvious reasons. The best in show was Mrs Billingham's nine-year-old Ch. Mahlib Jifft. A new-comer,

Mrs Johnson's Fashion of the Wells, ran through the bitch classes from novice upwards, to best bitch. Shortly after this Fashion went to South Africa with her owner and is the ancestress of many winning Dalmatians there today.

The year 1946 still saw no general championship shows, owing to benching and other difficulties, but many breeds were allowed by the Kennel Club to hold championship shows during 1946 and 1947. For example, the British Dalmatian Club held two such shows and the North of England Dalmatian Club one championship show, in 1946. In 1947 both clubs held two championship shows. In 1947 general championship shows were resumed to a limited extent.

The first post-war specialist championship show of the breed took place on 8 May 1946 at Tattersalls. It was run by the British Dalmatian Club, and was judged by Mrs Shirley Simpson and the late Mrs Beal; another was held in October, both very successful. The North of England Club held an open show in April 1946 and a championship show the following October, equally successful. Practically all exhibitors went to both shows. Each club also held two championship shows in 1947, by which time the general shows were beginning to be held, the first at Peterborough in the summer of that year.

And so at last we had some new champions. The first two to be made up were Miss Clay's Ch. Tantivvey Naomi and Mrs Bloomfield's Ch. Norseman of Welfield, litter brother and sister from Miss Clay's fine litter already mentioned. The other two champions in it were Mrs Parker's Ch. Tobias of the Towpath and American Ch. Nigel of Welfield, exported by Mrs Bloomfield to the United States.

Not all the new general championship shows survived, some faded away after their first effort, others struggled on for a time before they resigned themselves to the inevitable, but the old and tried championship shows of the past went on in general into the future with new momentum, and Dalmatian entries became increasingly good both in numbers and quality.

Fortunately we had a nucleus of good-class Dalmatians to

play their part in the improvement of the breed after the long interval of the war, when most of us were too busy with various forms of work to do much breeding. Those who were able to do so bred one or two litters in order not to lose their established strains and so there was continuity between the dogs of the pre-war period and those that came after. Many faults which had been present in some pre-war animals had become fixed because of indiscriminate breeding by novices. Such faults were upright shoulders in plenty, general poor conformation, light eyes, and other faults not recognized as serious by the inexperienced breeders. There was much to do in this respect. One difficulty was that puppies were at a premium and quite fantastic prices were asked and received for most indifferent stock. Neither buyers nor sellers, in many cases, really knew what a good Dalmatian should look like. This position gradually righted itself with the advent of shows judged by experienced judges.

The first post-war Cruft's was held in October 1948 by the Kennel Club, which had bought it from Charles Cruft's widow. October had been the traditional month for the Kennel Club's own show, not revived after the war, since Crufts had taken its place. The highlight of my own show career, if I may mention it here, was that my Ch. Winnall Elegance, daughter of my Winnall Joker, having won her sixth certificate at this first post-war Cruft's, survived into the last eight in the best in show ring. In those days, unlike today, every certificate winner in every breed appeared in the best in show ring and had to compete with every other certificate winner in all breeds, for the days of group judging had not yet arrived. This latter method is the most spectacular as well as being the most time saving and least exhausting both for exhibitor and exhibit. It builds up to an exciting and dramatic climax for everyone concerned when organized as it is at Cruft's.

But to return to 1949. No Cruft's show was held that year, after the October show of 1948, but from then on, with the exception of 1954, when a strike of the Electrical Trades Union forced a last-minute cancellation, Cruft's has been held at the traditional date early in February at Olympia each year and has grown in size and prestige throughout the years. It is by far the greatest and largest dog show in the world and well deserves its great reputation. To be invited by the Kennel Club to judge at Cruft's is the ambition of every judge.

As time passed the ever-increasing number of entries forced the organisers, the Kennel Club, to introduce a system of 'Qualifiers' whereby only dogs which had won certain specified awards at championship shows during the preceding season might be entered. Like most well intentioned legislation this ruling had its drawbacks, notably the pressure on exhibitors, and their dogs, to at all costs 'qualify for Cruft's' by entering for every show possible.

The other change which has taken place is the move from Olympia to nearby Earl's Court which provides slightly more spacious accommodation. There have been many calls for Cruft's to be moved altogether out of the congestion of central London and to a time of year when exhibitors might be free from the acute weather problems attendant upon a February date. So far the Kennel Club has turned a deaf ear to these pleas and while the public continue to flock to Earl's Court the cash value of the 'gate' will probably prevail.

But to return to those early post-war days; time went on, the old championship shows were revived, in many cases altered from their traditional dates, and Dalmatians continued to advance.

There was a slight recession in 1953–4; the post-war boom had worn itself out, but the little slump which succeeded it was quickly over and Dalmatians steadily improved, though they are still naturally far from perfect. Breeders became more experienced, and both clubs were active, the Northern confining its activities in the main to Manchester and its district, holding until recently two open shows annually. When the breed became entitled to two championship shows yearly, the Northern Club took one. Both now run a championship show yearly and a third joint championship show.

Two of the BDC's most successful and popular activities have been its newsletter, entitled Spots of News and its

Handbook. Mr Yeomans conceived the idea of a periodical for the club and his wife Madeleine Yeomans edited it brilliantly for eight years. Succeeding editors have been Miss Rita Monkhouse, Miss Mary Gatheral, Mrs Enid Aldrich-Blake and the present incumbent of the office, Mrs Marjorie Cooper. Unfortunately, the escalating cost of printing and postage obliged the club to reduce the number of issues from monthly to bi-monthly, a decision accepted as necessary by the membership but greatly regretted.

The club Handbooks, which are greatly prized, are produced every three or four years. The high cost of production prohibits annual editions but each volume continues the statistics and information where its predecessor left off so that there is an unbroken sequence. Such a record of breed history will ensure that future generations will have information about the breed, which has never before been available, years after the event. Illustrations of the leading dogs of the time will be especially useful.

In 1947 the President of the BDC, Mr Kemp died at a great age, having held office for twenty-two years. His successors were Miss Evelyn Barnes, Mrs Nixey, Miss Betty Clay – who later served as Chairman for twenty-five years – Dr Frankling and more recently Mrs Joan Agate-Hilton. The club has been most fortunate in having a number of dedicated and knowledgeable people in charge of affairs. Among the most deserving of mention are the hard-working Secretaries. Recent holders of this office have been Mr Charles Clover, Mrs Muriel Green, Mrs Gwen Eady down to the present secretary, Mrs Joan Curtis.

The North of England Dalmatian Club has continued to prosper. Following the death in 1961 of their much loved President Mrs Wigglesworth who had served the club devotedly for many years, her successors, who included Mr Fred Makin, Miss Monkhouse and Mr Herbert Essam have all made their own special contribution to the office. The current President is Mr A. E. Johnson with Miss S. D. A. Gatheral as Chairman and Mrs D. McKay as Secretary. A feature of the club is the excellent newsletter Carriage Dog Chronicle.

Mr Linley Byrd also gave many years of devoted service to

this club. Until his death in 1960 he occupied successively most of the senior offices, including that of Chairman. Mrs Byrd was the Northern Club's hard-working Secretary for a number of years. The present secretary is Mr F. S. Willis.

During the post-war years the British Dalmatian Club has grown steadily in stature and reputation. Its membership has increased considerably and its influence has spread so far afield that members are to be found in most parts of the world. It has members in Holland, France, Germany, Norway, Sweden, Belgium, Switzerland, and Italy.

Farther afield the British Dalmatian Club has members in the United States of America, Australia, South Africa and the West Indies. In the United States, in addition to the Dalmatian Club of America, there are no less than twelve regional clubs.

These overseas members maintain friendly relations with the British Club. All receive the Newsletter and the Handbooks. It is doubtful whether any British dog club has so many foreign and overseas members, and it is something of which we can be very proud.

The British Dalmatian Club maintains its vitality and its capacity for growth and progress. As older members die or become less active, new ones take their place and it is remarkable how many of these there are, seriously interested in the breed and all that concerns it.

It would be invidious to mention the names of the prominent breeders of today. These will be found in Appendix C which gives the names of all the post-war champions to date, with their owners, breeders, parents, and date of birth.

Certain prefixes, among them those of comparatively recent standing, are already household words, to be relied on for sound and typical stock.

Mere numbers, whether of club members, breeders, exhibitors, registrations, or show entries, count for little. These provide the basis for progress in a breed, but knowledge and experience has to be gained before either a useful contribution can be made to a breed or lasting personal success can crown the breeder and his stock. And there are no short cuts.

Modern Dalmatian history would be incomplete without

a mention of Dodie Smith's enchanting book, *One Hundred and One Dalmatians* (1956), and the subsequent cartoon made from it by Walt Disney which appeared in 1961.

If one book delighted thousands of readers the film appealed to thousands more, and it is extraordinary how, in some subtle way and in this medium, Disney managed to capture the essence of the Dalmatian.

There is no doubt that both book and film played a part in rousing interest in the breed on the part of the general public.

Dalmatians have mercifully remained free from the worst kinds of commercialism; the majority of breeders love the breed for its own sake and long may this remain so. Such breeds as ours are not seriously threatened by every wind of change that blows, that may well bring disaster to less ancient and well-established breeds. Dalmatian fortunes are based on something much more fundamental and lasting.

3
The Standard and Its Evolution

It is in comparatively recent times only that breed standards have come into being. As we have seen, opinions on the appearance of breeds have been expressed for centuries, and the ideal Dalmatian has been variously described according to the personal ideas of the writer. These ideas naturally differed with individual tastes and the views of the period in which they were written. None of them was official. Indeed, until the establishment of authoritative canine organizations such as Kennel Clubs or other ruling bodies, and breed clubs, there could be no official standards. Our own Kennel Club, the fore-runner of all others, was founded in 1873.

With the subsequent formation of breed clubs in this country it became necessary to issue formal statements describing ideal specimens of the various breeds, and these were the first official standards. They were compiled by the breed clubs concerned.

Even up to 1947 standards remained the concern of breed clubs only. These clubs had multiplied within many breeds, some of which had more than twenty. From this the anomalous situation arose whereby every club within a breed could, and often did, have its own standard and standards often differed considerably from club to club.

With the rivalry, not always friendly, which grew up between competing clubs within a breed, especially the more 'popular', the situation can be imagined. It often happened that judges on any one club's list were almost automatically unacceptable to its rivals. This state of affairs led neither to consistent judging nor consistent breeding, and in 1947 the Kennel Club decided to put an end to it by unifying the standards of all its recognized breeds. It called on all clubs within every breed, through the medium of each breed's elected representative to the Kennel Club Council of Representatives, to consult together and to agree on a single standard acceptable to them all. These standards were issued by the Kennel Club as its own official breed standards in 1950. They are binding on clubs and cannot be altered without the consent of the Kennel Club. This is always given when reasonable grounds exist for the change.

Happy the breed with few clubs, among which was our own, for by this time two only were in existence, the North of England Dalmatian Club, the senior, and the British Dalmatian Club by far the bigger, and with a large foreign and overseas membership.

I speak of this process of unification with some experience as breed representative, for, though my task was not easy, agreement between the two clubs was reached in the end by a compromise. A shorter, more concise standard is in use today.

Queries are constantly made about standards, and how they should be arrived at. How flexible they should be or how rigid; how separate points should be evaluated in relation to one another; whether dogs can fairly be judged by a numerical standard of points. Such queries are endless and there are as many opinions as questions.

A breed standard can be described as an attempt to define in detail an ideal specimen of a breed. This attempt will be more or less successful in proportion to the knowledge and clear-mindedness of those who draw it up, and, one must add, their power of putting their views clearly and concisely.

A standard is a pattern to aim at, not a formula to which every dog must conform exactly to be considered a worthy specimen of its breed. And as the perfect dog has yet to be born we must not expect even the best dogs to fulfil every single requirement of the standard. No written standard can define or contain everything that goes to make up the perfect dog. There are always the imponderables; that outlook, that poise, that bearing which belongs to the true champion can be recognized instantly by those with an eye but cannot be fully described in words.

The true champion should possess personality, that indefinable quality which stands out in a crowd, which distinguishes its owner from the mass. Not all champions add up to this ideal, even *near* perfection of points does not necessarily endow the possessor with it. It depends on character and temperament to a great extent. It is inborn and cannot be acquired. Dogs of this calibre stand out permanently in the memory of all who have been fortunate enough to see them.

We must now consider in detail those unofficial Dalmatian standards which were compiled before the first official standard, that of 1890.

As we have seen in Chapter 1, these standards were fairly numerous during the second half of the nineteenth century and they were collectively the source from which the 1890 standard emerged.

That great dog man Vero Shaw drew up the first formal description under systematic headings. It was included, with others, in his *Book of the Dog* published in parts by Cassell, Petter, Galpin & Co. over a period up to 1882.

After discussing the breed in general, as described in Chapter 1 of this book, Shaw gives the requirements for different points and finally a numerical standard of points by which the dogs should be judged, as follows:

The Dalmatian or Coach Dog (1882)
The Head of the Dalmatian should be wide and flat, blunt at the muzzle and tight-lipped, nose black.

Ears rather small, V-shaped and very fine. If these are well spotted great beauty is added to the dog's appearance.

Eyes dark and inclined to be small.

Neck arched and light, tapering on to powerful and sloping shoulders.

Chest deep and rather broad.

Body round in ribs and well ribbed up behind.

Forelegs straight and very muscular; plenty of bone is essential in this breed so as to enable the dog to stand the wear and tear he has to encounter on the hard roads he is compelled to traverse.

Feet round, with the toes arched and well split up, pads round, firm, and elastic.

Hind Legs muscular with clean hocks placed near the ground as in the Bulldog.

Tail tapering from the root and carried as a Pointer's, this must be well spotted.

Colour and Markings well spotted all over with either black- or liver-coloured spots or both. These should not intermingle and should be of the size sixpence to a halfpenny.

Coat is close and fine.

General Appearance is that of a strong, muscular dog, capable of enduring considerable fatigue and possessing a fair amount of speed.

The scale of points by which these dogs should be judged is as follows:

General Appearance	10
Colour, Markings, and Coat	25
Neck, Chest, and Body	5
Head, including Ears and Eyes	5
Legs, Feet, and Tail	5
Total	50

This, on the whole, is not a bad standard and even today one cannot find fault with many of its provisions. Some, however, are open to criticism. To describe the head merely as 'wide and flat', without mentioning length or strength of muzzle, gives a wrong impression to anyone who does not know the breed.

'Body round in ribs and well ribbed up behind' – The first part of this clause draws no distinction between the moderately rounded ribs of the 1890 standard, which we still like, and the barrel ribs which are not typical of the breed and which are indeed a physiological handicap. I wish that we had the second part of this clause today because it stresses the length of chest with resulting room for lung expansion and the absence of a long, weak gap between the last rib and the pelvis. Vero Shaw mentions sloping shoulders for, I believe, the first time in any description of the breed.

The clause on the tail calls for comment. At this time the Dalmatian, as we have seen, was considered ideally to be as like a Pointer as possible, in fact the tail of the Pointer was metaphorically grafted on to the Dalmatian. But this tail carriage, tail stretched rigidly in a straight line with the back, is not correct in our breed. Dalmatian tails should be carried with a slight upward curve, though never curled.

Under 'Colour and Markings' we have now decreed that black and liver spots on the same dog are faulty. Since all our dogs today are descendants of those of the nineteenth century, and we cannot lay the responsibility on animals imported from elsewhere, it is not surprising that this fault occurs from time to time, even now. More will be said on this point when dealing with Dalmatian inheritance.

The description of coat is better than that of today, and if the word 'short' were added it would be entirely adequate.

And so we come on to the next comprehensive, though still unofficial, standard, that of Stonehenge (Walsh) in the fifth edition of his book *Dogs of the British Islands* published in 1886. And though in his first book *The Dog* Walsh had classified our breed among what are now sporting dogs, 'domesticated dogs finding game by scent but not killing it, being chiefly used in aid of the gun', both in the second and fifth edition he alters this classification to 'Non-Sporting Dogs, in the Watchdog Group', with St Bernards and others.

Walsh's standard in this fifth edition of *Dogs of the British Islands* runs as follows:

'The following is the Numerical Value of the Points of The Dalmatian' (1886)

Head	10	Legs and Feet	10	Coat	5
Neck	5	Tail	5	Colour	10
Body	5	Symmetry	10	Markings	40
	20		25		55

Grand Total 100

1. *The Head* (value 10) exactly resembles that of the Pointer but so long as the nose is cleanly cut under the eyes and square at the point, great breadth is not insisted on and there should be no flews. The ears should not be long and hound-like but flat, thin, and vine-shaped,

lying close to the cheeks and rather smaller than those of the Pointer. Eyes small, dark, and brilliant.

2. *The Neck* (value 5) should be arched like that of the Pointer, without any throatiness or approach to dewlap.

3. *The Body* (value 5) must be moderately strong but not heavy and lumbering; sloping shoulders and a muscular loin are imperative.

4. *In Legs and Feet* (value 10) the Dalmatian ought to be perfect, as his sole employment is on the road; very strong bone, however, is not demanded, as he has no shocks to withstand, and useless lumber of any kind is to be deprecated. However, straight limbs united with elbows well let down and clean hocks form the desideratum in this breed. The *Feet* must be strong and close, whether hare- or cat-like, and the horny sole should be regarded of necessity as thick and tough.

5. *The Tail* (value 5) should be small in bone after it leaves the root, and should be gently curved in one direction only, not with any approach to a corkscrew twist.

6. *The Symmetry* (value 10) should be examined closely and if deficient penalized accordingly.

7. *In Coat* this dog resembles the Pointer in all respects, being short without any approach to silkiness.

8. *The Colour* (value 10) is either black, liver, or dark blue. Sometimes there is a stain of tan about the head and legs which is not objected to. A clear jet black is more highly valued than black-and-tan, and liver and blue being of equal value.

9. *The Marking* (value 40) is the point on which the judging of this breed mainly depends, some breeders valuing it at 50 out of the 100. I cannot, however, think that a well-marked cripple should prevail over a moderately well-marked dog perfect in all other respects and I have consequently lowered the value of this point to 40. In no case should there be a black patch on any part of the body or head exceeding the size of half a crown, and the nearer the spots approach to the size intermediate between a shilling and half a crown and to the circular shape, the higher the estimate made. None should be smaller, if possible, than a shilling, but no dog has ever yet appeared without a few such 'flecks' or 'freckles'. A well-spotted tail is greatly admired but is very rarely met with. The white ground should be quite distinct from the spots, without any approach to freckles on it and the more regularly the spots are distributed the better. It is usual to divide the valuation of the several qualities in the markings as follows: size 15; shape and well-defined edges 15; regular distribution so as to avoid patches 10.'

Clearly the word 'Patch' had not then the sinister con-
notation it has today. The Pointer comparison is still
stressed according to the fashion of the time and it must be
admitted that in the illustration of a couple of Pointers in
the same book, there is not a great deal of difference
between the two breeds, apart from the large pendulous
Pointer ears and the markings. Walsh's Pointers have no
pronounced stop, no dish faces (that incurved line from eyes
to tip of muzzle), no deep, square jaws, and no loosely fitting
lips.

Walsh also mentions sloping shoulders and it seems likely
that he drew on Vero Shaw's descriptions, though he did not
always agree with them. One would imagine, for instance,
that a dog which ran miles under a coach or carriage would
certainly experience a certain amount of shock from the
many times repeated contact of pads with the highway, even
though not the heavily metalled roads of today. The brief
clause on symmetry is not enlightening and Walsh himself
might have been hard put to it to explain exactly what
he meant.

Dark blue is mentioned as a permitted colour in this standard and it would be immensely interesting to know what
colour is meant. When describing colour in some animals,
'blue fox' for instance, blue is not that of ordinary shades as
known in colour cards or flower colours, but a sort of silvery
fawn. The late Lord Wrottesley registered a dog as blue in
1930, and I must have seen this dog, but do not remember
anything unusual in its colour.

Walsh has some wise words to say on the relative value of
decoration and structure. These are not out of date even
today. Dalmatian decoration is so spectacular that it is
fatally easy for the novice judge, or for that matter the
novice breeder or exhibitor, to concentrate on this point
alone. No expert knowledge is needed to assess it.

Very rightly Walsh stresses the importance of correct
structure and soundness in his standard. He also mentions
good feet 'whether hare- or cat-like', the only occasion, I
believe, on which hare feet are approved for the breed.

Little else calls for comment in Walsh's standard. It is difficult to believe that his views are based entirely on his own experience which, according to his other writings, appears to have been slight. But by this time dog books were becoming more common, Dalmatians were more or less fashionable, and information about them was more easily obtained than at any time in their history.

And now we come to yet another unofficial standard and this time a foreign one. In his *Dalmatian Handbook* Mr Clifford Hubbard gives an interesting piece of Dalmatian history, previously unknown to me. It is that of a standard suggested for use by the first Dalmatian Club of 1890 by Mr Hugo Droesse, a prominent enthusiast of that time and the first Secretary of this club. It is a translation of a standard which appeared in *Der Hunde Sport*, the date of which is not given. It was published in English in *The Fancier's Gazette* in 1889 and reads as follows:

Size, Shape, and Weight. That of a small Pointer.

General Appearance. A fine, lively, uncommon dog, fine and muscular form, which must be neither lumpy nor weak.

Head. Resembling that of the Pointer, but not so deep or broad in the nose. Nose dry, skin tight, lips not overhanging.

Eyes. Smallish, round, and full of spirit. An intelligent expression should be present. In those spotted black, the eye must be black, blue-black, or brown in different tints. In those spotted brown, all colours, yellow inclusive, but not black.

Eye-rims. Black in black-spotted, brown in brown-spotted but not flesh-coloured.

Ears. Placed higher than the Pointer and not so big but moderate. Broad below and well rounded at the ends, V-shaped, thin and fine.

Nose. In black, black. In brown, brown.

Neck. Moderately long, well built, elegant, light, and free from foul.

Shoulder. Slanting, strong, and muscular but not heavy, nevertheless elegant and built for speed.

Breast. Pretty broad and deep.

Hindquarters. Elegant, strong, but not heavy; ribs well sprung, neither round nor barrelled, as would give the appearance of sloth.

Legs. Of the greatest importance; straight and muscular but not too strong, elbows well tucked in, toes well together and compact (cat-footed), soles horny and hard, hind legs muscular and hocks like a Pointer, the stifles behind and before straight and bony.

Nails. In black, black or white, in brown, brown or white.

Tail. Strong and bony at the set-on, fining down almost immediately and ending very fine, with a curve but not curled; always spotted, the more the better.

Skin. Tight, but allowing the muscles to show well.

Hair. Short and close, smooth and not rough, never silky or woolly.

Colour Description. Ground colour always pure white, never silver-grey or yellow. The spots in the black-spotted must be black, the darker the better. In the browns, brown with black spots. Spots from one shilling to half a crown in size, nearly circular, showing off well, well divided, not too close together, not allowing too large a space of white to appear, not freckled.

Scale of Points

Build and Symmetry	20
Colour, Hair, and Spots	20
Head and Expression	9
Spotted Ears	4
Neck and Breast	10
Legs and Feet	15
Forequarters	8
Hindquarters	8
Spotted Tail	6
	100

I should have liked to see the original of this standard to be able to see how good a translation it is but have been unable to get any information on it.

The description of the nose as 'dry' is puzzling. This term is used on the Continent to describe a neck free from loose skin or throatiness as we call it.

The clause on ears is bad and confusing, but reference to the original might have made it clearer.

The chest is well described, possibly the best comment we have seen so far, though rather strangely included in *Hindquarters.*

The stifles are poorly described and 'close-fitting' would have been a better word to describe the skin. Nowadays a 'tight' skin in a Dalmatian implies poor condition.

Mixed colouration is again allowed, though to accept black spots on a brown dog but not brown on a black dog is odd, because the latter must have been more common. In fact I do not think I have ever seen a liver dog with permanently black spots. Nor have I seen a picture of a fundamentally brown dog with black spots, though plenty exist of black dogs spotted also with brown.

This seems to be the first standard to mention nails and their colour and the clause could well have been omitted, or, if included, the important point of shortness could have been stressed. No doubt the compilers of the actual 1890 standard took the point about nails from this earlier foreign attempt.

And so at last we come to the first official breed standard, that of the Dalmatian Club founded in 1890.

The Dalmatian in many respects resembles the Pointer, more especially in build and outline, though the markings peculiar to this breed are a very important feature and very highly prized.

In General Appearance the Dalmatian should represent a strong muscular and active dog, symmetrical in outline, free from coarseness and lumber, capable of great endurance combined with a fair amount of speed.

The Head should be of fair length, the skull flat, rather broad between the ears and moderately well defined at the temples, i.e. exhibiting a fair amount of 'stop', and not in one straight line from the nose to the occiput bone as required in a Bull Terrier. It should be entirely free from wrinkle.

The Muzzle should be long and powerful, the lips clean, fitting the jaw moderately close.

The Eyes should be set moderately well apart and of medium size, round, bright, and sparkling with an intelligent expression, their colour greatly depending on the markings of the dog; in the black-spotted variety the eyes should be dark (black or dark brown); in the liver-spotted variety they should be light (yellow or light brown). The rim round the eyes in the black-spotted variety should be black, brown in the liver-spotted variety, never flesh-coloured in either.

The Ears should be set on rather high, of moderate size, rather wide at the base, tapering to a rounded point. They should be carried close to the head, be thin and fine in texture, and always spotted, the more profusely the better.

The Nose. The black-spotted variety should always be black, in the liver-spotted variety always brown.

Neck and Shoulders. The chest should not be too wide but very deep and capacious; ribs moderately well sprung but never rounded like barrel hoops (which would indicate want of speed); the loins strong, muscular, and lightly arched.

Legs and Feet are of great importance. The forelegs should be perfectly straight, strong and heavy in bone, elbows close to the body, forefeet round, compact, and well arched. Toes cat-footed and round, tough elastic pads; in the hind legs the muscles should be clean though well defined, the hocks well let down.

Nails. In the black-spotted variety, black and white; in the liver-spotted variety, brown and white.

The Tail should not be too long but should be strong at the insertion, gradually tapering towards the end and free from coarseness. It should not be inserted too low down but should be carried with a slight curve upwards and never curled. It should be spotted, the more profusely the better.

The Coat should be short, hard, dense, and fine, sleek and glossy in appearance but neither woolly nor silk.

Colour and Markings. These are most important points. The ground colour in both varieties should be pure white, very decided and not intermixed. The colour of the spots in the black-spotted variety should be black, the deeper and richer the better; in the liver-spotted variety they should be brown. The spots should not intermingle but be as round and well-defined as possible, the more distinct the better; in size they should vary from that of a sixpence to a florin. The spots on face, ears, legs, tail, and extremities should be smaller than those on the body.

Size. Dogs 55 lb. Bitches 35 lb.

Standard of Excellence

Head and Eyes	10
Legs and Feet	15
Ears	5
Coat	5
Neck and Shoulders	10
Body, Back, Chest, and Loins	10
Colour and Markings	30

Tail	5
Size and Symmetry	10
	100

The difficulty of compiling numerical standards and their doubtful value in assessing the relative importance of various points is obvious and will be considered in due course.

We must now jump thirty-five years for any significant alteration in this standard. The North of England Club at its foundation in 1903 adopted the existing standard in its entirety except for an alteration in the size of bitches from 35 lb to 50 lb.

When the Southern Dalmatian Club was founded in 1925 it made three alterations to the existing standard, as it was then entitled to do without the agreement of the senior club, or the Dalmatian Club itself, already in decline. The new club followed the Northern Club in its wise action in the size of bitches, increasing their weight to 50 lb, but it deleted the Pointer comparison, still dear to the heart of the Northern Club. And it omitted the statement that the eye-rims should never be flesh-coloured. It rearranged the order and content of some clauses but without altering them in essentials.

Dalmatian Standard 1968
Reproduced by permission of the Kennel Club.
  General Appearance. The Dalmatian should be a balanced, strong, muscular and active dog, of good demeanour, symmetrical in outline, free from coarseness and lumber, capable of great endurance with a fair amount of speed.
  Head and Skull. The head should be of fair length, the skull flat, reasonably broad between the ears, but refined, moderately defined at the temples, i.e. exhibiting a fair amount of stop, not in one straight line from nose to occiput bone, entirely free from wrinkle. The muzzle should be long and powerful, the lips clean, fitting the jaw moderately close. The nose in the black-spotted variety should always be black, in the liver-spotted variety always brown.
  Eyes. The eyes, set moderately well apart, should be of medium size,

round, bright, and sparkling, with an intelligent expression their colour depending on the markings of the dog, dark in the black spotted, in the liver-spotted variety always brown. The rim round the eyes should be complete, dark in the black spotted, liver brown in the liver spotted.

Ears. The ears should be set on rather high, of moderate size, rather wide at the base, tapering to a rounded point, fine in texture carried close to the head. The markings should be well broken up, perferably spotted.

Mouth. The teeth should meet, the upper slightly overlapping the lower. (scissor bite)

Neck. The neck should be fairly long, nicely arched, light and tapering, entirely free from throatiness.

Forequarters. The shoulders should be moderately oblique, clean and muscular. Elbows close to the body, forelegs perfectly straight, with strong round bone down to the feet, with a slight spring at the pastern joint.

Body. The chest should not be too wide but deep and capacious, with plenty of heartroom. The ribs well sprung and well defined withers, powerful level back, loins strong, clean and muscular and slightly arched.

Hindquarters. Rounded, muscles clean, with well developed second thigh, good turn of stifle and hocks well defined.

Tail. In length reaching approximately to the hocks. Strong at the insertion, gradually tapering towards the end. It should not be inserted too low or too high, be free from coarseness and carried with a slight upward curve, never curled, and preferably spotted.

Feet. Round, compact, with well arched toes (cat feet), and round, tough, elastic pads. Nails black or white in the black-spotted variety, in the liver spotted, brown or white.

Gait. The Dalmatian should have great freedom of movement, a smooth, powerful rhythmic action with a long stride. Viewed from behind the legs should move in parallel, the hind legs tracking the fore. A short stride and a paddling action is incorrect.

The Coat. Should be short, hard, and dense, sleek and glossy in appearance. The ground colour should be pure white. Black-spotted dogs should have dense black spots and liver-spotted dogs liver brown spots. They should not run together but be round and well defined, the size of sixpence to half a crown as well distributed as possible. Spots on the extremities should be smaller than those on the body.

Size. Overall balance of prime importance but the ideal to be aimed at is:

Dogs 23–24 inches. Bitches 22–23 inches.

Faults. Patches, black and liver spots on the same dog (tri-colouration). Lemon spots, blue eyes, bronzing and other faults of pigmentation.

The Dalmatian Standard in this country has never before had a standard of height in the Dalmatian, and it is difficult to understand why. We now have a revised and much improved standard which does include height.

It is obvious that rigid figures are not needed and that slight differences on either side of this standard are acceptable.

Occasionally a member of the Club wishes to stick to the one figure, but rigid figures play no part in living creatures and this cannot be accepted.

As the result of great advances in the knowledge of nutrition during the past forty years, the dogs of today are better fed than ever before and this should not be forgotten when considering the well-being of the dog.

Weight has been omitted in the standard and with good reason, for it is a variable depending on a number of circumstances such as feeding (quality and quantity), exercise, treatment of dog by owner and so on, none of which can be rigid and unalterable.

One criticism often heard about this standard is the word 'moderate'. It is constantly used; 'shoulders moderately oblique', 'eyes moderately well apart', and so on. Opinions differ strongly on this question. Can it be that the breeders of those days had a good deal more knowledge of animals in general, and particularly the horse, than most of our breeders today, some of whom live in a sort of vacuum with their Dalmatians, having no standards of comparison with other breeds.

The breeder with more general interests seeing a point described as moderate, ears for instance, visualizes the Pointer's ears as examples of large size in a not dissimilar breed. The one-breed man asks helplessly: 'What is moderate?'

Opinions will always differ on the value of exact measurements. Those with mechanical minds believe them to be needed. Those concerned rather with the behaviour of living organisms think that too rigid an insistence on weights and measures in living animals, on exact figures for every detail of structure after the fashion of an architect's plan, will result in neglect of less-easily assessed features. Dogs may gain high awards because they conform to exact measurements and have no outstanding faults. They may be equally devoid of outstanding virtues.

The English are said to be a nation of pragmatists. They believe in what has been found to work, even though academically it should not do so. This is nowhere more clearly shown than in our doggy activities. Our present system of judging Dalmatians has worked for over seventy years. It has been used in such a way by breeders and judges that extremes and exaggerations have been avoided and that, though faults still exist, a steady improvement has come about. We should think carefully before substituting a more mechanical system.

As we have seen, the Numerical Standard of Points became a prominent feature of assessments of the breed during the latter part of the nineteenth century, and remained in force until 1950, though as a yardstick for judges it had become a dead letter. Attempts to use it showed marked differences of opinion among the writers of earlier days. Whether or not all tried it in practice is not revealed. Stonehenge certainly did. Had judges followed this system some remarkable results would have occurred, and perhaps they did. In many people's opinion the Kennel Club made a wise decision when it decided to delete all numerical standards from its official breed standards.

In 1985–6 the Kennel Club instituted a review of all Breed Standards, in consultation with the breed clubs. Lengthy discussions ensued and on some points agreement was reached only with difficulty. The final draft for the Dalmatian was completed in 1986 and is reproduced below.

General Appearance. A distinctively spotted dog, balanced, strong, muscular, active dog. Symmetrical in outline, free from coarseness and lumber.

Characteristics. A carriage dog of good demeanor, capable of great endurance and a fair turn of speed.

Temperament. Outgoing and friendly, not shy or hesitant, free from nervousness and aggression.

Head and Skull. Of fair length, skull flat, reasonably broad between ears, moderately well defined in front of ears. Moderate amount of stop. Entirely free from wrinkle. Muzzle long, powerful, never snipey; lips clean, fitting jaw moderately closely. Nose in black spotted variety always black, in liver spotted variety always brown.

Eyes. Set moderately well apart, medium size, round, bright and sparkling, with intelligent expression. Colour, dark in black spotted, amber in liver spotted. Eye rims preferably completely black in black spotted, and liver brown in liver spotted.

Ears. Set on rather high, moderate size, rather wide at base, gradually tapering to rounded point. Fine in texture, carried close to head. Marking well broken up, preferably spotted.

Mouth. Jaws strong, with a perfect, regular and complete scissor bite, i.e. the upper teeth closely overlapping the lower teeth and set square to the jaws.

Neck. Fairly long, nicely arched, light and tapering. Entirely free from throatiness.

Forequarters. Shoulders moderately oblique, clean and muscular. Elbows close to body. Forelegs perfectly straight with strong round bone down to feet, with slight spring at pastern joint.

Body. Chest not too wide but deep and capacious with plenty of lung and heart room. Ribs well sprung, well defined withers, powerful level back, loin strong, clean, muscular and slightly arched.

Hindquarters. Rounded, muscles clean with well developed second thigh, good turn of stifle, hocks well defined.

Feet. Round, compact, with well arched toes, cat-like, round, tough, elastic pads. Nails black or white in black spotted variety, in liver spotted, brown or white.

Tail. Length reaching approximately to hock. Strong at insertion gradually tapering toward end, never inserted too low or too high, free from coarseness and carried with a slight upward curve, never curled. Preferably spotted.

Gait/Movement. Great freedom of movement. Smooth, powerful, rhythmic action with long stride. Viewed from behind, legs move in parallel, hindlegs tracking the fore. A short stride and paddling action incorrect.

Detail from *The Congress of Münster*, 1647, by Gerard ter Borch

Hunting Dogs and their Attendants, by Francesco Castiglioni, circa 1776

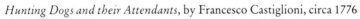

Kitty Coaxer driving Lord Dupe towards Rotten Row, by John Collet, circa 1770

The Legend of St Hubert, by Heinrich Wahl, 1750

The Coach Dog, by Reinagle, 1803

Hackney and Dalmatian Dog in Landscape, by J. N. Sartorius, 1819

The Duke of Devonshire on the Box of his Four-in-hand, by C. H. Seaforth, 1869
(There are three Dalmatians shown in this painting)

Pongo, following his traditional occupation, with Mr and Mrs Sanders-Watney,
winning the Driving Championship, Hickstead, July 1963

Coat. Short, hard dense; sleek and glossy in appearance.

Colour. Ground colour pure white. Black spotted, dense black spots, and liver spotted, liver brown spots; not running together but round and well defined. In size one pence to fifty pence piece. Spots as well distributed as possible. Spots on extremities smaller than those on body. Patches, tri-colours and lemon spots highly undesirable. Bronzing on spots undesirable in adults.

Size. Overall balance of prime importance. Ideal height: Dogs 58.4–61 cm (23–24 ins). Bitches 55.9–58.4 cm (22–23 ins).

Faults. Any departure from the foregoing points should be considered a fault and the seriousness with which the fault should be regarded should be in exact proportion to its degree.

Note. Male animals should have two apparently normal testicles fully descended into the scrotum.

Temperament. Temperament is an abstract concept and its results can be observed in the behaviour of the dog. Like every other feature, it is the result of the external events we call environment on the hereditary pattern of the individual concerned.

Temperament is one of the features often ignored by dog breeders and this is a pity, for the best and most beautiful dog in the world is useless if it displays a bad temperament.

The history of its earliest days must be known if the puppy's temperament is to be assessed, for pups display their budding characters early in life.

Much poor temperament in pups is caused, not necessarily from neglect or cruelty, but because of the total absence of communication between breeder and puppy in its early stages in life. The foundation of all good relationships should be established early.

The number of puppies which suffer from hereditary nervousness is far fewer than the pups which owe their nervousness to the behaviour, or lack of it, of the humans who should be their friends.

Puppies which, from birth, suffer from a pathological nervousness and which shrink from all human contacts and live in a state of irrational fear are the victims of hereditary nervousness which, from its very nature is incurable. These unfortunate victims of chance should not, in mercy, be allowed to survive. Their condition is pitiable and permanent.

The Dalmatian which is the companion of its owner becomes almost capable of reading his thoughts and the breed is most affectionate and obedient. Some dogs have a charming habit of bringing a 'present' to their human friends after even the shortest absence from home. This may be a bone, a toy, a duster, in fact anything handy. They also have a smile which wrinkles up their noses and displays their teeth. This is often taken by the uninitiated to be a snarl. In reality it is a mark of the greatest affection. They would defend their owner if necessary as the writer has experienced.

The bitches are very good mothers and usually have big litters which may well present a problem. No bitch should be allowed to keep more than six or seven puppies. Any with defects, which is not common, should be put down at birth and weaklings should be painlessly destroyed, preferably by a veterinary surgeon.

The sale of surplus puppies should be just as carefully considered as to a suitability of the homes they are going to as are the best in the litter.

Unfortunately commercialism is rife and in many cases breeders are not concerned with the future well-being of the puppies they produce and will sell to anyone who will pay the price with no questions asked.

Dalmatian breeders, and especially those who belong to the Clubs, are not included in this category. The bulk of club members combine in the dogs the functions of pet dog, show dog and close friend in a single animal.

Much research on canine behaviour has been carried out in the United States by dedicated scientists and their conclusions on the behaviour of puppies is most interesting. The conclusions are that a great deal of nervousness and unsatisfactory behaviour in the adolescent puppy is the result of the absence of the normal sequence of events in the life of the very young puppy.

Such instances as very early weaning in order to bring a bitch back to the show ring, and using artificial means to bring a bitch on heat only six weeks after the birth of her last litter, in total disregard of the well-being of either bitch or puppies. The result of the latter attempt is not known, but the callousness of those who engineered this attempt will be remembered.

The breed has become popular, the last thing that the dedicated Dalmatian lover would wish.

4

The Uric Acid Problem

Before food substances can be utilised by the body they must be broken down into simpler substances by the action of enzymes. These are natural chemical substances, each with its own specific reaction, that causes changes in other substances without themselves undergoing any change.

Food proteins are normally broken down to the stage of a substance called allantoin, of which uric acid is the precursor. This condition is a physiological anomaly and not a disease. The human being, the anthropoid apes, and the Dalmatians stop short in their protein metabolism at the stage of uric acid. Whether or not all Dalmatians are affected we do not know, but it is highly improbable, for the majority appear to be free from this trouble. Many strains do not suffer from symptoms of it while other strains are afflicted and pass on the condition regularly to their offspring.

Two as yet unproved theories for this anomaly have been put forward; the first is that the enzyme uricase, normally present in the liver, is totally absent in the liver of a Dalmatian. The second is that the uric acid passes so rapidly through the renal tubules that no conversion of uric acid has time to occur.

Marca Burns, in her excellent and interesting second edition of *Genetics of the Dog*, goes some way in elucidating this problem.

She writes, 'The Dalmatian appears to be less able than other breeds to break down uric acid into allantoin, which causes the excretion of a large amount of uric acid in the urine. This peculiarity does not seem to have any serious effect on the animals, although Dalmatians are reported to be slightly more susceptible to kidney stones than are other breeds (Keeler 1940). The characteristic high uric acid excretion behaved as a simple Mendelian recessive in crosses between Dalmatians and other breeds (Trimble and Keeler 1938), and segregated independently of the spotted coat colour characteristic of the Dalmatian. They also have fewer intranuclear crystals in their liver cells than have other breeds; this condition is inherited and appears to be associated with high uric acid excretion (Weatherford and Trimble 1940). Harvey and Christensen (1964) report that the erythrocytes of the Dalmatian appear to lack the mediated transport system for uric acid which can be demonstrated in the erythrocytes of other dogs. This is apparently another manifestation of the genetic peculiarity of this breed.'

The diet of a dog suffering from excess uric acid should be very low in protein, some of which should be vegetable.

Those Dalmatian lovers who have an intimate knowledge of the breed may be surprised to hear of all the handicaps which apparently beset it. In spite of this Dalmatians are normally hardy and healthy and the dogs usually live to a ripe old age, some even to fifteen years old, with few troubles. Many breeders, of which the writer is one, cannot believe that every Dalmatian dog is afflicted in this manner though undoubtedly a number are. The condition is clearly hereditary and probably a recessive one; it is passed on in some breeds with apparent regularity, but in others not at all. It is only recently that any treatment other than that of a surgical operation to remove stones from the urinary tract has been available to cope with this problem.

This has now been solved in the United States. Mr John C. Lowrey, a dedicated lover of Dalmatians and an able scientist, has founded a research establishment for his interesting work on dogs, and especially the Dalmatian, as well as further projects.

One of his Dalmatians, Fred, had already undergone four operations for kidney stones and was selected for the first trial of a drug called allopurinol. The dog was given this drug regularly for a considerable period, well over a year. He showed no signs of uric acid trouble and no side effects ensued. Doses have to be given daily. Fred has had no further trouble and is displaying no symptoms of any. Burroughs Wellcome and Co. (USA) produce this drug. It is now recognised by the authorities as suitable for this purpose and it is thought that it may soon be used for human patients.

Mr Lowrey's next objective is the investigation of deafness which we hope will be successful, after the rather negative results of the Swedish scientists' work on this subject.

Allopurinol is now available in Britain under the trade name 'Zyloric'. It has proved helpful in treating certain kinds of kidney disease involving an excess of uric acid. It is a most expensive drug.

There are now available for use in conjunction with veterinary treatment various ready-prepared complete diets which should help owners in caring for dogs with renal problems.

In 1980 the Animal Health Trust's Small Animals Hospital near Cambridge undertook a four-year study of chronic renal disease in dogs under Dr D. F. McDougall. Some twenty-five veterinary practices were invited to co-operate in the study by supplying material and reports and by sending patients for treatment. Much useful information regarding diagnosis and treatment was compiled. Early diagnosis and strict attention to diet emerged as being prime factors in successful treatment.

More recently an Oncology Unit has been set up under Dr L. Owen to study the increasing number of cancers appearing in dogs. So far results have been encouraging but further funding will be needed to enable the Unit to extend its lines of research. There is a free exchange of information with those engaged in research into human cancers, to the probable advantage of both.

5
Dalmatian Character and Conformation

DALMATIAN CHARACTER

What kind of a dog is a Dalmatian? What can the buyer of a Dalmatian puppy expect to get for his money? First, something without price; the love of a good and faithful companion in good days and bad; a dog obedient and easily trained from puppyhood onwards, with a life span of eleven years or more during which time his owner may expect freedom from serious illness provided that the precautions available today against infections are taken and the dog is well fed and cared for.

Dalmatians are natural unspoilt animals, they suffer from none of the disabilities of structure not uncommon today.

A Dalmatian, even if not in the top flight as far as shows are concerned, is still a striking and attractive animal of which his owner can be proud.

No elaborate preparation is needed before this dog can be shown, if this is the owner's ambition. He will have a trouble-free dog which, if it is good enough, can become famous in the history of the breed. It can give its owner not only a delightful hobby but hosts of good friends, and the chance of helping to pay for its own costs of living. Dalmatians are not, however, recommended as money spinners for the commercially minded.

The typical Dalmatian is gay and friendly, gentle in temperament, with none of the toughness which makes some breeds difficult to train. A severe scolding is usually the greatest punishment required, and it reduces the dog to apology and often abasement. Though not strictly a one-man dog, for it maintains friendly relations with the entire household and is especially good with children, there is usually one person to whom its first allegiance is owed.

71

Dalmatians are not aggressive dogs, and do not look for trouble, but are able to cope with it if necessary, and are exceptionally good guards.

Human companionship, to some degree at any rate, is needed to develop Dalmatian character and usefulness to its fullest extent. It delights in work of any kind, obedience, the country pursuits of ratting or rabbiting, and gundog work to which several of my dogs have been successfully trained, for it has an excellent nose and a soft mouth. It is intelligent, quickly learning the meaning of a large number of words and phrases. It is well aware of what it is doing and of the doggy crimes it commits, it knows just what it wants and how to get it and it has a sense of humour.

The present day pattern of home life where in many cases both partner are out at work for most of the day does not provide a satisfactory life for a Dalmatian puppy. If they are to become congenial companions they need from the first kindly and regular training and supervision and, most of all, human companionship. Dalmatians are very much 'people's' dogs. Far too many young adult dogs which end up on the books of one of the Rescue societies are the victims of this lack of early training. If people are not able to provide a proper home life for a puppy they would be wiser to postpone having one until more favourable circumstances prevail.

Owners of large kennels obviously cannot keep all their dogs in the house, but regular human contacts, other than feeding and putting out to exercise, are essential for the Dalmatian to make the most of its capabilities. As a housedog and companion it is second to none, and combines this most happily with a show career as the owners of many famous Dalmatians would be happy to testify. Close relationship with its owner as a companion leads to a mutual trust and understanding which makes dog and master a single unit, working in the closest co-operation, in the showring as well as outside.

There are those who proclaim their dogs to be all but human in intelligence. This is not the case, for the dog does not possess many of the attributes of humanity, though it is free from its uglier vices. It has memory, and Dalmatian memory is long, but it has no fear of the future, no knowledge of death and for this we can be thankful. But, without falling into the heresy of anthropomorphism, we can still believe that the dog is no mere bundle of conditioned reflexes. I am convinced that dogs have some primitive reasoning power of their own and are capable of forming elementary concepts. This I have found in many of my own dogs by actions which could not have been the result of experience, instinct, or association. Many scientists nowadays, including Sir Julian Huxley, have come to believe this; dog lovers found it out for themselves long ago.

Experiments on animals behaviour are carried out mainly on laboratory animals, that is animals living in abnormal conditions. However well they may be treated, as of course they are, they are of necessity deprived of many activities which are an essential part of the life of a normal free dog. One would hardly expect the reactions of such dogs to be a true indication of the mental processes of those living in more natural conditions.

But however well one knows one's dog and its personality, there is inevitably a part of its life which even the most devoted owner cannot share. Its mental processes are on a different plane from our own, and even its senses, especially those of hearing and smell, function in a range far beyond those of humans, giving the dog, as it were, another dimension in which to live where we cannot join in. It is in fact a dog and must remain so, and its reactions cannot be foreseen in all circumstances.

And yet how marvellously well this alien creature has adapted itself to human lives in the course of evolution, to develop so many qualities of mind and temperament, and to share with us the joys and sorrows of our lives. Our responsibility for the welfare and happiness of our dogs is correspondingly great.

And yet, with all its near-human qualities, a group of dogs not controlled by man will form themselves into a pack with its own leader, though singly, dogs accept their owners as their pack leaders.

In character the typical Dalmatian is an extrovert, friendly to all except intruders, anxious to please, taking life as it comes, affectionate and loyal, not a complicated character one would say, and best controlled by patience and the mutual affection between owner and dog.

There is no more satisfactory companion, and as a show dog all these qualities stand it in good stead. The typical Dalmatian enjoys shows, and likes to show itself off – a ring full of them with every tail waving and every dog cheerful and gay is a splendid sight. Dalmatians usually lie quietly on their benches, a watchful eye on things around them, always alert for the return of an absent owner. In fact this dog takes everything in its stride with equanimity and good temper, and the occasional dog which resents passers-by or other dogs only shows off the good behaviour of the large majority.

DALMATIAN CONFORMATION

The standard tells us what a good Dalmatian should look like, but we need to translate words into pictures and to see the dog in three dimensions to understand it fully. The standard is an abstract conception, the dog is a concrete fact, consisting of a skeleton which includes bones of all sizes and shapes, jointed to one another by various mechanical methods, the loose ball-and-socket joint of the shoulder, the strong tight ball-and-socket of the hip, the hinge of the knee, and so on.

There is nothing haphazard about the arrangement, it is common to many species and has been evolved to perform as perfectly as possible the functions necessary to life and health.

The skeleton is clothed in muscles, which are attached to bones and joints and give rise to movements of the various parts of the body by their system of alternate flexion and extension. This system is controlled by the brain which transmits electric impulses to the muscle fibres by a complex system of nerves, large and small, running throughout the body. The central nervous system recalls irresistibly a power-station with its vast network of high-tension cables and wires. It is a voluntary system, controlled by the will. Another and involuntary system exists in the body, outside the control of the will and functioning throughout life to maintain all the vital processes, respiration, circulation of the blood, digestion, reproduction, and all the many physiological events of a lifetime.

Soundness, in its widest sense, includes the whole body with its complex structure and functions, all of which should work harmoniously and efficiently. As applied to dogs, soundness is often confined to locomotion.

The Dalmatian is a strong upstanding animal of medium size, conveying an impression of substance combined with elegance of outline and perfect balance. Its bony structure is ideally suited not only to easy action but to all the vital processes of life. A chest which allows the fullest possible expansion which speed or endurance could demand; a back strong, short-coupled, compact, and free from weakness; shoulders, hip-joints, hocks, and stifles so angulated as to make possible free, effortless action which is both elegant and economical, and a pelvis constructed for easy whelping, are the inheritance of the Dalmatian. In fact a dog of this breed, conforming precisely to the standard, is perfect in conformation from every point of view.

The Head needs little comment; it is well balanced with a capacious skull and a powerful, long muzzle.

The Spine is the most important group of bones in the body. Unlike that of the horse it is extremely flexible, and this can be seen in any Dalmatian at full gallop when the spine arches almost into a hoop and the hind legs overtake and pass outside the forelegs in the stride.

The spine consists of twenty-five hollow segments called vertebrae containing the spinal cord. The first group of seven, the cervical, support the neck. The thirteen dorsal or thoracic, so called because with the thirteen pairs of ribs attached to them they form the chest or thorax, containing the heart and lungs. The next five are the lumbar, in the loin region, and behind these lies a solid bone called the sacrum, made from fused vertebrae, which forms the upper side of the pelvis and leads to the coccygeal bones of the tail.

The pelvis is a kind of basin with a front inlet and a rear

1. Dalmatian outline

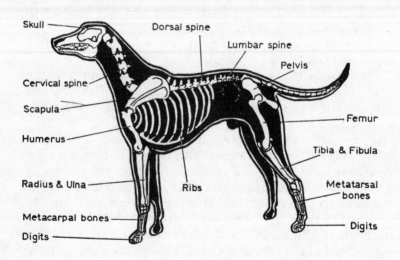

2. Dalmatian skeleton

outlet. The bones forming it are the ilium (hip bone), the ischium, and the pubis, the foremost and lowest.

Pelvic structure has considerable bearing on whelping. Should the pelvis be deformed from rickets or accident, natural whelping is likely to be difficult or impossible.

It will be obvious that the length of neck, chest, and loin will depend on the length of their respective vertebrae.

The cervical vertebrae curve from the base of the skull to their junction with the next group, giving the graceful arched neck so desirable in the Dalmatian. Should they be short, the neck will be short and in consequence the shoulder-blades (scapulae) which lie over the forward three thoracic vertebrae will be placed still farther forward, resulting in an angle between neck and body instead of the flowing line it should be.

Long thoracic vertebrae are also desirable for upon their length the length of the rib cage depends. 'Heart room' is often mentioned as needed in dogs. No dog is ever likely to suffer for lack of it; the heart is small and needs little space to accommodate its beat. Lung room, however, is another matter. Should the rib cage be short, which would be the case with short thoracic vertebrae, there would be little room for the chest expansion needed in exertion or when breathing is hampered, as in pneumonia. A chest with a long rib cage is described as 'well ribbed-up', or 'well ribbed-back', giving plenty of room and this should be a feature of the Dalmatian.

The lumbar vertebrae on the other hand should not be long. If they are, a long space between the last rib and the pelvis occurs which is a source of weakness to the back and loin. What in show-ring terms is 'a long back' is more often a long loin, as the result of a short rib cage.

Ribs in the Dalmatian should be neither barrel-shaped nor flat. They should be gently rounded, giving the possibility of maximum expansion when required. The dog's ribs expand laterally rather than antero-posteriorly as in man. A barrel chest is already fully expanded and cannot respond to increased demands due to exertion; an overflat chest lacks to some extent the capacity to expand. Neither the

3. Well-laid shoulder (*above*) and upright shoulder (*below*)

excessively rounded nor the flat and meagre chest is correct in Dalmatians, and it should not be shallow, its lowest point, the brisket, should be at elbow level.

The Forequarter. The scapulae (shoulder-blades) lie over the first three thoracic vertebrae on either side, and approach each other, with a small space between them, in the middle line of the back. They should be fairly long and sloping in the Dalmatian. The shoulder-blades are attached to the ribs by muscles only, their only bony attachment is at the shoulder-joint where they articulate with the humerus.

The standard demands a 'moderately oblique' shoulder. This is one in which the angle between humerus and scapula is roughly 90 degrees, a right angle. The humerus slopes backwards from the shoulder-joint to the elbow-joint which lies well behind the shoulder and is tucked against the chest wall. The two lower bones of the foreleg, radius and ulna, should be vertical and parallel from the elbow to the ground. This conformation allows the forelegs to move forward with a long stride, covering a good deal of ground. The forelegs must be parallel both standing and in action, the feet must not turn in or out.

It will be obvious that with an upright shoulder the humerus will lie in a more upright position, the forward swing of the forelegs will be shorter and the elbows farther forward and not so well under the body, action will be less easy and the forefeet will be turned in.

The difference between the placement of an upright shoulder and an oblique shoulder, as well as its result in action, can be seen by observation at any dog show and are illustrated.

The radius and ulna (the lower bones of the foreleg), extend from the elbow to the pastern-joint, which corresponds to the human wrist. This part of the foreleg lies at an angle with the upper arm, but is itself vertical and the two forelegs should be parallel with each other, and should have the width of about two legs between them. The terrier front, in which the forelegs are close together, 'coming out of the same hole' as it is sometimes called, is quite wrong in the Dalmatian. The pastern-joint is straight, but with a slight

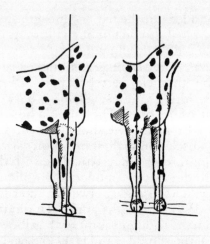

4. Forelegs parallel and straight

5. Hindquarters powerful, legs parallel,
hocks and stifles moderately bent

'give', allowing a degree of flexibility when the leg comes
down hard on the ground as in galloping and above all jump-
ing. This flexibility acts as a shock absorber for the dog in
the same way that bent knees do in a parachute jumper. A
straight leg could cause serious fractures of the limbs.

The region between the pastern joint and the dog's paw
corresponds with the human palm, and the dog's feet, both
fore and hind, consist only of toes, on which it walks. Dew-

claws are rudimentary thumbs, and, like the human thumb, do not lie in the same plane as the other digits.

The Hindquarter. Dalmatian quarters should be strong and not narrow over the loin, and the outline of well-developed muscles should be seen clearly on the buttocks and legs. The lower leg, commonly called the second thigh, should also be well muscled. Only exercise will give this beautiful modelling and the animal with flat quarters and weak leg muscles tells its own story to the knowledgeable eye.

The hip-joint should be angulated after the fashion of the shoulder-joint, with about a right angle between the pelvis and the femur. This is a stronger joint than that of the shoulder. The head of the femur is practically spherical and is enclosed in a deep cup-like cavity called the acetabulum, formed by the union of the three paired pelvic bones, ilium, ischium, and pubis, all of which take part in the joint. The head of the femur is attached within the acetabulum by a powerful ligament, allowing movement within the joint capsule which consists of strong fibrous tissue enclosing the head and joint cavity securely.

A malformed, often flattened, head of the femur, or an unduly shallow or deformed acetabulum, or a combination of the two, constitute hip dysplasia, an hereditary disease hardly known in Dalmatians and to be avoided at all costs.

The femur is jointed to the lower leg at the stifle-joint, corresponding to the human knee. A kneecap, or patella, lies over the joint in a slight groove in the bone which holds it in place. I have never heard of a slipping patella in Dalmatians, though an unstable kneecap is an hereditary defect in some breeds of dog.

The stifle should be moderately well bent, without the extreme angulation of the Alsatian or the straightness of the Chow Chow. A straight stifle limits the forward thrust of the hind legs, which gives propulsive power, and causes the stilted gait which is correct in the Chow but quite wrong in the Dalmatian. The hock-joint corresponds with the human heel; it connects the tibia and fibula with the metatarsal bones, corresponding to the sole of the human foot and should be well, though not excessively angulated. The hind legs, like the fore, should be parallel in stance and action. A hock which turns in is described as a cow hock, which explains itself to anyone who has seen a cow walk. The hind feet are rather more oval in shape than the fore, they should not turn in or out.

The Dalmatian's tail is set-on fairly level with the back line, neither high nor low. It must not be coarse, and never curly. It is carried with a slight upwared curve, sometimes described as a sabre tail.

The general impression of a Dalmatian is one of a dog combining substance with elegance and avoiding the two extremes of coarseness or over-refinement, of slightness or heaviness in build, having no one feature exaggerated but presenting a harmonious whole. It should appear capable of carrying out its old function as a carriage dog or its even older role as a sporting dog. Its balance and proportions should satisfy the eye and give a sense of perfect harmony both in repose and action.

6
Choosing a Puppy

The choice of the first Dalmatian, whether as pet, show dog, or breeding stock, or happily a combination of the three, is a momentous one for the new enthusiast.

The advice that follows will, it is hoped, be useful not only in the choice of the first puppy but in the subsequent decision as to which to keep from the litters the potential breeder looks forward to eagerly.

The possibility of future breeding is one of the reasons for starting in Dalmatians with the best stock available, though the pet owner will also want an animal he can be proud to own.

It is on the whole true that the best and most successful breeders have the best stock. They are known for their successes in the show-ring and for the quality and health of the stock they sell to other breeders and exhibitors; in many cases their reputations are such that they have waiting lists for puppies and hardly need to advertise. Reputable breeders can be relied on to deal fairly with the novice, and they prefer the prospective buyer to see their stock before deciding on a puppy. A knowledgeable friend can always be taken to help in the choice.

From six to eight weeks is a good time to choose a Dalmatian puppy, for an idea can then be obtained of its probable appearance as an adult. It is less easy to assess during the awkward stage of adolescence a couple of months later. The most, however, that can be said of any young puppy is that it is really promising. The puppy which looks well balanced at eight weeks almost always returns to this stage. Moreover at this age puppies are already individuals, each with its own character, tendencies, and possibilities, each needing individual care and attention. A litter which remains a litter too long becomes a pack and the important early training is perforce postponed.

Should breeding be contemplated it is better to start with a bitch puppy or perhaps two, and the best should be the aim as far as possible. The first step towards breeding has then been taken. A dog should not be acquired at this early stage for the services of the best can be had for a fee. Dalmatians are not among the breeds which command extremely high prices and bitches are the heart of a breeding kennel.

Another and important reason for starting with good animals is that the first is probably the most important in its owner's career, for it is the beginning of his education in the breed. It will become the pattern of a Dalmatian in his mind; if he is attached to it, as indeed all Dalmatian owners are, it will be the yardstick of merit until he has gained experience. How important then that the pattern should be as perfect as possible, for the eye accepts as normal what is constantly before it and it is better to start with an eye trained to what is correct and harmonious than to have to adjust later.

Whatever the future may hold for the novice it is best to start with stock from a well-known kennel where breeding is taken seriously. Pedigrees are all-important, but only in so far as the dogs named in them are known as individuals, with their virtues and their faults. A pedigree sprinkled with the names of a dozen or more champions may be of little breeding value though it impresses the uninitiated.

One in which the name of a single animal occurs several times, famous not only for a show career, but for the merits of the stock it has produced, is more likely to breed good puppies than one with a haphazard assortment of champions, however numerous they may have been, or famous as individuals.

The novice who is fortunate enough to start with a first-class animal begins a show career with everything in his favour, though he may be tempted to forget that even his paragon has faults. The most important thing is not that his dog wins prizes, but that his own eye is educated from the beginning to recognize and appreciate excellence.

WHAT A GOOD DALMATIAN PUPPY SHOULD LOOK LIKE
Shape gives the impression of squareness, the length of the back from the withers to the set-on of tail is about the same as the height from withers to the ground.

Body is rounded, never long and skinny, the chest reaching to the elbows at its lowest point, the brisket; the ribs are well rounded, neither they nor the spine should project. The underline shows a slight arch in the loin though this is not so marked as it will become with maturity; the shoulder placement is easily seen if the pup can be persuaded to trot but is obvious in any case to a trained eye, the upright shoulder is easily recognized by the fore-hand action. There is no pot-belly or hernia.

The back is level from behind the withers to about the set-on of tail, it should not dip behind the withers nor should it roach.

The *Legs* show good bone and should not appear fragile; even at this age feet are round and toes arched, thin, flat spreading toes are a bad fault and little can be done to correct them.

The *Head* is well modelled with a defined stop, ears are small and neat and carried close to the head; eyes are round, bright, and clear, the darker the better in black-spotted puppies, in livers the eyes should be light brown, golden, or amber. Pale eyes are not attractive. At birth puppies' eyes, like those of babies, are blue, pigment is laid down only later and eyes may darken at least up to a year or more. Pigmentation of the nose and eye-rims may not be complete at this age though a good deal of colour is normal, often in small separated areas which should have joined up to a great extent. Unpigmented areas which are a dusky bluish pink with a blurred line dividing them from the pigmented portions are almost certain to colour over completely; bright-pink areas with a definite line of demarcation between them and the pigmented portions are less likely to become covered with pigment; jaws are neither heavy nor snipey; a Roman nose in a young puppy is often the sign of future length and strength of muzzle. Teeth are not easy to assess at this age; if the upper lip covers and rests on the lower and the milk teeth are in correct alignment the permanent teeth are likely also to be correctly aligned. A lower jaw protruding beyond the upper is a danger signal and may mean undershot teeth in the permanent dentition.

The *Skin* should be loose and supple, the coat bright, never staring or rough.

Spotting. The perfect spotting described in the standard is rare even in adult dogs. In puppies the final pattern is not complete though general over- or underspotting will be seen at this age. A fairly well-covered puppy is preferable to a very lightly marked one, and any completely unspotted areas on body or limbs will show up even more clearly with maturity. Completely black ears are not desirable.

No responsible breeder sells a patched puppy.

The *Tail* carriage is uncertain at this age, teething or worms can cause a temporary curling, even excitement can send the tail up. A tail curled over the back is unlikely to correct itself later.

Temperament, that most important feature often neglected in favour of other show points, is as necessary to the show dog as to the pet, perhaps even more, for the show winner of bad temperament is likely to be bred from and will perpetuate his defect. Heredity plays a large part in temperament though environment in the shape of outside circumstances can deface or destroy a good hereditary pattern. Bad handling, cruelty, neglect, or failure to bring about a happy relationship between dog and human, all these can affect the temperament.

The typical Dalmatian puppy is gay, friendly, forthcoming, bold, lively, and active. It is not timid or scared, it approaches people with confidence, and does not flinch from an outstretched hand or sudden movement.

Confidence, once destroyed, takes a long time to reestablish. In possessing and looking after dogs, owners need just as much, sometimes even more, training than the animals they acquire, sometimes so lightheartedly.

The new puppy is a responsibility, and everything must be done to help it to settle down in its new home well and quickly.

It will miss its companions if it is alone, but should have its own bed and sleep in it from the beginning. An old fur glove or a bundle of woolly rags tied together will give it something to creep up to during the first few lonely nights. Training is dealt with in the next chapter.

7
General Management and Training

'Half the Pedigree goes in at the Mouth'. This was a saying well known to breeders of an earlier day. Though not of course literally true, it is a striking way of stating a truth which they recognized though with no such evidence for it as we have today; the truth that the best inheritance must be reinforced by an environment which permits its full development.

Nutrition is probably the most important factor in general management as far as young animals are concerned; it is the basis of health, and food suitable in quality and quantity is the first subject to consider.

Good nutrition involves a supply of the basic food elements in adequate amounts; protein, carbohydrate, and fats, with the essential vitamins and mineral salts, including the 'trace' elements, needed in minute amounts but essential to the proper functioning of the animal body.

This body can be thought of as a giant factory, taking in food as its raw material and by complicated chemical processes reducing it to the simpler forms which can be absorbed and utilized. Thus proteins are reduced to the smaller number of amino-acids which form the building material of all body structures, carbohydrates (starches and sugars) to the simpler forms of sugar, of which glucose is the most easily absorbed. This is converted into glycogen and stored in the liver, to be released as needed. Fats are broken down into fatty acids by the presence of bile.

Although the first vitamin (Vitamin D) was discovered only in 1915, a large number are now known. They are substances found in natural foods or synthesized in the animal body, the presence of which, in small quantities, is essential to health. Their absence can cause specific diseases as well as general malnutrition. Their importance is generally recognized today and their functions interlock in some cases.

Vitamins A and D are probably the most important in the growing period. Vitamin A is important for night vision, it gives resistance to infection, and assists in normal growth of the tissues. It is found in cod- and halibut-liver oil, egg yolk, animal fats, carrots, and most green vegetables. It arises from the breakdown of a plant pigment, Beta Carotene. Vitamin D (often associated with A) is needed for good bone and teeth, it prevents rickets. It is formed in the skin by the action of sunlight and is found naturally in fish oils, butter, and eggs. Vitamin B comprises a complex series of different chemical substances many of which overlap in some functions though they are specific in others. They may be said to act as a team and a shortage of one is likely to upset the balance of the complex. A whole-yeast preparation contains most if not all of the already discovered group. Liver, wheat germ, and egg yolk are normal sources. Vetzyme is a useful preparation of the entire series. Vitamin C is called the anti-scurvy vitamin. It occurs in green vegetables and most acid fruits, especially the citrus group. Dogs normally synthesize this vitamin for themselves, though cases of inability to do so have been recorded.

Vitamin E is called the fertility vitamin though its value in this respect has been queried. It is useful for its action on the heart muscle. Vitamin K is needed to enable the blood to clot.

Minerals necessary for health are lime and phosphorus in a certain ratio, iron, manganese and other trace elements, zinc, cobalt, and iodine.

Dogs are naturally carnivorous but with domestication they have become adapted to a mixed diet. If the dog could eat its natural food all necessary food factors would be included; it would live on the animals it killed and its diet would include skin, bones, internal organs such as kidney, liver, and intestines as well as muscle meat. In these days of processing, preserving, dehydration, refrigeration, subtractions and additions of all kinds, dogs may well go short of some essentials. Those fed on table scraps and biscuits are most likely to suffer, though the advent of the wholemeal biscuit and biscuit meal has solved some problems. Meat, in all its forms, should play a large part in the diet of a healthy dog, and the internal organs such as liver should not be forgotten. Tripe is excellent.

To sum up: from conception to death the tissues of the animal body are first built up, then maintained and repaired by the food materials supplied by the bitch during pregnancy and lactation and later by the dog's own food. Good condition, good health, and vigour depend on food of the right amount and the right quality. Just as the increased knowledge of nutrition of the past fifty years has improved the size, health, and stamina of children, so it has with dogs whose owners have kept abreast with modern knowledge.

FEEDING THE YOUNG DALMATIAN

We shall consider puppy feeding in Chapter 9. At about three months the adolescent period begins, when height tends to increase at the expense of substance and the pup may become lanky and rangy as puppy fat disappears and well-developed muscles have not yet rounded off the skeleton.

Moreover the permanent teeth begin to erupt during the fourth month and the mouth may become sore which means reduced-food intake. As regards teething, an examination of the mouth should be made if any puppy goes off its food at about this age. Most often an erupting tooth will be seen. Should the milk tooth be still firmly embedded when a permanent tooth erupts alongside it, the veterinary surgeon should be asked to remove it. Most often the milk teeth fall out easily, and when loose a small amount of pressure from the finger will ease them out, for they have no roots.

Good feeding is essential during this period, and amounts must be increased.

The food supplements should still be used. Cod-liver oil and malt are sometimes helpful in loss of appetite.

During this period too the bones are calcifying, that is, lime is being laid down in the bone substance. Puppies should never be allowed to get too fat, for weight in excess may cause bending of bones still far from hard. Too much hard exercise is also a mistake at this time, though exercise there must be to develop the muscles. Muscular development has a great deal to do with correct action.

Lack of Appetite. It has been emphasized that Dalmatians normally have good appetites, but a case of poor appetite occurs occasionally, especially in young dogs. These often become normal with maturity but in the meantime nutrition may suffer. A dog which refuses food for a day or two will not necessarily become hungry as time goes on. Eating too little becomes a habit as easily as does eating too much. It is sensible to do everything possible to break the habit in its early stages. Dogs vary considerably in the amount of food they need and this should not be overlooked.

'Appetite comes with eating' and if the reluctant Dalmatian can be persuaded to eat a mouthful or two, it may end by eating the entire meal. Competition is valuable in some cases and a greedy dog at hand may induce the difficult dog to ensure that the second dog does not deprive him of his rights.

I think perhaps it is true to say that a spoilt Dalmatian may sometimes behave as a spoilt child and enjoy the attention caused by his refusal of food.

In any case every effort must be made to get the dog to eat. A day or two of reduced food, however, will not hurt any healthy dog and I have found that the 'broody' bitch often refuses food for several days, but makes up for it when she becomes normal. Persistent refusal of food is another matter.

By the age of seven or eight months two good feeds daily including at least a pound of meat, with perhaps a little milk, are enough. All the supplements should be given. Although by this age the skeleton has nearly attained its adult size a great deal of muscular development has still to take place. The dog has to 'make up' as we say and exercise is an important factor in this development.

FEEDING THE ADULT DALMATIAN
Opinions differ on the number of meals which the fully

grown Dalmatian needs daily. My own have always been fed twice. The first meal is a light one, consisting of wholemeal biscuits, or biscuit meal soaked in soup from the dog pot, with a small amount of meat or fish added and an egg yolk from time to time. Any good meaty table scraps or green vegetables are added to this with Vetzyme tablets and cod- or halibut-oil in cold weather or if there is any lack of fitness. This meal is given after the morning walk which is an extensive one with a good deal of free running in addition to road work.

The last meal is given in the evening and consists of meat, roughly a pound, cut into good-sized pieces. The dog does not chew its food. As the shape of its teeth indicates it swallows everything in large lumps, and since its gastric juice is very strong in hydrochloric acid it is wise to give this plenty to do. It is significant that when meat and biscuit are fed at the same meal, the biscuit remains in the stomach long after the meat has been digested. This is proved by the occasional vomit.

Vegetables in the diet is another matter which provokes discussion. Most Dalmatians will eat cooked green vegetables, also raw chopped spinach or cabbage, but my experience is that it has to be so well mixed in with a tasty meal that it goes down with the rest. The young twitch grass which all dogs look for so eagerly when grass begins to grow in the spring ought to have some value. It is certainly not always eaten to cause vomiting, though grass often is eaten for this purpose.

The lengthy chopping up of this and that herb in specified amounts seems to me to have little value.

Changes of food can be made from time to time to add interest and variety to the menu but most Dalmatians enjoy their food and are not at all fussy. They are certainly the easiest to feed of any breed I have owned.

FEEDING THE OLD DALMATIAN
The appetite of a healthy old dog does not flag with age, and I have found the main problem to be that of preventing such a dog from eating too much, and especially starchy food.

Elderly Dalmatians tend to put on weight, often, I think, because their owners cannot resist their pleading eyes.

It is no kindness to allow any dog to become seriously over-weight. Every bodily function is handicapped, and notably that of the heart. Exercise is slow and difficult because of the unwieldy body, breathing may be embarrassed, life may be shortened. Even in the extreme old age which our Dalmatians often attain, exercise should not be abandoned altogether. This is often the highlight of the old dog's day.

EXERCISE

From the old dogs we return to puppies. Up to eight weeks or so pups get all the exercise they need in play with their companions and this is often extremely rough and vigorous. Plenty of space must be allowed for it. It is the birthright of all young things and should not be denied them for any reason. It is sad to think that modern farming methods now deprive numbers of young animals of a normal life from birth to an early death.

The normal rhythm of puppyhood is play, sleep, food. It is most important that rest should be part of every puppy's routine; this point should be stressed to all who buy young puppies, especially those with young children. In fact I regard the attitude of 'a plaything for the children' as ominous for the well being and happiness of any puppy.

Children tire of puppies as quickly as they tire of any other toys, and treat them in some cases just as ruthlessly. Even the well-intentioned child may be too young to know that puppies must not be hurt and need a lot of rest.

A solitary puppy in a new home will miss the family rough and tumble and some other form of play and exercise must be provided. Eight weeks is rather too early for systematic road exercise, apart from the fact that puppies are best kept off the road until they have had their inoculations.

The owner must be prepared to give time to playing with the puppy unless he is fortunate enough to be able to call on sensible children to do this for him. A kitten and a puppy of about the same age often get on well together, though they must be introduced with care. A solid rubber ball of the right size, that is one which it is quite impossible for the puppy to swallow, is a useful toy, and a solid rubber ring is also popular. Spratts make an excellent and quite unchewable solid ball in various sizes.

The owner of any puppy, whether pet or potential show dog, must face the fact that a puppy is a responsibility which cannot be placed on other shoulders. He ignores this responsibility at the peril of the pup's happiness, habits, even life. Puppies can be introduced to road exercise as soon as they have learned to walk reasonably sensibly on the lead. They should never be allowed loose on a road.

Exercising the adult Dalmatian. Exercise is not only essential for a dog's happiness but for its health, and free running must be part of the day's routine as well as walking on a lead. It has already been stressed that only exercise develops the body and its muscles to the strong, elegant, well-modelled shape of the good Dalmatian. It also stimulates all the bodily functions which depend on muscular action, the bowel in elimination, the uterus in whelping, the heart in maintaining circulation, the chest wall in breathing. Flabby internal muscles mean flabby organs.

It is difficult to overtire a well-developed full-grown Dalmatian by any normal means if it is accustomed to plenty of free running. Dogs which have freedom to play with companions and live with a family, with access to garden or paddock, naturally need less exercise than the dog confined to a kennel for much of its time. But every dog should have daily road exercise, it will harden pads, wear down nails, and so bring the dog up on the toes. It may even prevent a tendency to spreading feet if taken in time, by ensuring that nails are short.

Adults may be allowed to run with a bicycle for short distances, but the pace must not be faster than the brisk trot which is characteristic of the breed.

The ideal and traditional exercise for the Dalmatian is to follow a horse and their instincts for this are still unimpaired. One sees this delightful sight seldom nowadays, but at least one Dalmatian is still to be seen following its traditional occupation at some of our big horse shows. The recent upsurge of interest in horse and pony riding means that a few fortunate Dalmatians are able to enjoy using their ancient instincts.

The lot of a Dalmatian deprived of vigorous exercise and condemned to loaf about in a small run for most of its time with no opportunity for stretching its legs in a good gallop is a sad one. They thrive on exercise and work.

HOUSING

The large kennel will need permanent buildings. The ideal building material is brick which is hardly dearer than wood today and has the advantage of being warmer and safer if any form of heating is used. Electric heating is undoubtedly the safest and a convector heater in a corner, well screened with wire netting and with the switch out of reach of dogs, is the ideal. The wiring must of course be up to standard and properly installed.

Wooden benches, well raised from the floor, make excellent beds with ledges to retain the bedding, the best form of which is wood wool.

Kennel buildings should be light and airy, runs and kennels should be kept thoroughly clean. Dalmatians are naturally clean dogs and dislike dirt intensely. Fresh clean water should always be available.

When large numbers of dogs are kept a kennel kitchen is a necessity, but Dalmatians are not usually kept in large numbers and two or three can live in the house with no trouble at all. However, a separate whelping/puppy kennel is always useful when breeding is carried on, a dual-purpose building which will house litters and be useful at other times when dogs have to be excluded from the house for any reason.

The House Dog. This description can be applied to the majority of our show Dalmatians as well as to the many pets. The house dog should always have its own bed to which it can retire at any time and in which it sleeps. A movable bed is the most useful for it is a good idea to move the sleeping place from time to time and this may be a convenience for the owner, as well as teaching the dog to accept as his sleeping place any room in which his bed is installed. There are many makes of good dog beds on the market; Goddards, one of the pioneers in this field, are still as good as any; their beds have the advantage of portability, so that if the dog goes away with its owner, its accustomed bed can go with it. A folded blanket on this bed makes it extremely comfortable.

GENERAL ASPECTS OF TRAINING

Apart from specialized training, which is outside the scope of this book, general training is essential for every dog. Even the dog intended only for the show-ring has much to learn apart from ring behaviour.

Training not only teaches the dog to be a good companion, it enables it to develop its own character and capacities, and, by no means less important, it ensures that the dog shall be a welcome member of the community in which it lives.

In fact one may say that a completely untrained Dalmatian, in common with dogs of all breeds, is not only an anxiety to its owner and at odds with its own instincts, but a nuisance to the neighbourhood in which it lives as well as being home-made propaganda for those who dislike dogs.

The dog was originally an animal which lived in packs, owing allegiance to the pack leader and submitting to the discipline and obedience of pack life.

Our domesticated dogs still need a substitute for this ancient tradition of behaviour, they need the discipline of authority and are happier for this. Many dogs today have none. However, the framework of a regular routine, with the recognized authority of a master (the modern pack leader and accepted by the dog as such), provides a settled life with a stable background. The unhappy dog, like the unhappy child, never knows what is going to happen next.

It is the owner's duty to undertake the task of training the dog and arranging its life on an orderly basis. He must be the master and the source of authority. He must never be a tyrant. Owner and dog both have lessons to learn, the one of understanding, the making the dog understand, patience

Ch. Snow Leopard, 1927 (*Thomas Fall*)

Ch. Lucky James, 1930, son of Ch. Snow Leopard (*Thomas Fall*)

Ch. Gwen of the Wells, 1936 (*Hedges*)

Ch. Cabaret Copyright, 1938 (*Hedges*)

Ch. Colonsay April Jest (*Anne Roslin-Williams*)

The author judging at the Three Counties Show, June 1962, with Mrs Aldrich-Blake's Ch. Illyricum Catriona Fraama and Mr R Finch's Ch. Merithew Hey Presto (*C.M. Cooke*)

Ch. Washakie Othello (*Diane Pearce*)

Ch. Greenmount Golden Guinea (*Thomas Fall*)

and consistence combined with authority and firmness, the other of obedience and submission to his master's will, which must, however, never be exercised unreasonably or irresponsibly. No sensible owner wants his dog to be reduced to the status of an automaton. It has a mind, and training should develop this rather than subjugate it. Authority must not be used merely from a desire to dominate, but only in the best interests of the dog.

In fact ownership of a dog entails also a discipline for its owner and a sense of responsibility both to the dog and the comunity, unfortunately not always recognized.

Happily our Dalmatians are in most cases the friends and companions of their owners who both love their dogs and recognize their responsibilities towards them.

REWARDS AND PUNISHMENTS

There is little or no place for punishment in the training of a young dog. In Dalmatians, which are usually anxious to please and are by no means tough, punishment during training is out of place and likely to do more harm than good. This breed like others has a simple mind by comparison with human standards and the trainer must make clear to the dog exactly what he wants it to do. Commands should be given in a firm voice and in the shortest terms, a single word if possible, which should always be the same for the same command. Dalmatians understand very quickly such simple commands as sit, come, go, stay, wait, and pick up other more complicated phrases without difficulty.

Rewards bulk large in the early stages of training. They may consist of a word of approval with a friendly pat; something more tangible is often useful and any delicacy can be given when the command has been obeyed. The dog trained in this way provides the perfect example of the conditioned reflex. Even the rustle of a piece of paper in the pocket which once held boiled liver provokes the instant response of alerted attention.

Dalmatians form habits with great rapidity and as habits once formed are hard to break, the importance of acquiring good rather than bad is obvious.

With these general remarks we can now go on to forms of

training needed for all dogs. The first and most obvious is house-training.

HOUSE TRAINING

Dalmatians are exceptionally easy to train to be clean in the house. In fact we often say that they are born practically house trained. The young puppy can begin to be trained at four or five weeks by the method of putting it outside immediately after every meal. In bad weather a tray or shallow box filled with sawdust can be used, and the pup should be lifted on to this as soon as it has finished its food.

The natural rhythm in infancy is for the entry of food into the stomach to set up a chain of reactions in the intestine which contracts and moves the contents on to be expelled from the bowel. This will not be the food just taken, but the residue of the previous meal. As the pup grows the rhythm will become less frequent until in adult life it is confined to one or two evacuations a day.

When a new puppy is taken into the house a little concentrated attention will be needed for a short time if successful house training is to be as rapid and perfect as possible. But no puppy can be expected to remain dry during an entire night and the tray of sawdust will be used if the pup has been trained to this.

The most important point in house training is to avoid all accidents. Once the smell of urine is present it is a powerful stimulus to the puppy to repeat the offence in the same place. This scent is difficult to get rid of and the dog's nose is much more efficient than the human variety.

In most cases puppy training is the prerogative of the female sex, and the trainer must keep the puppy with her as much as possible during the first week or two of house life. By watching one can anticipate trouble. At the first sign of squatting the pup should be picked up, taken outside and not left alone until it has relieved itself. If put outside and left, it will almost certainly wait by the door until it is opened and pass water as soon as it gets inside. This stage lasts for a very short time, unless the puppy is allowed to use the house for this purpose. This procedure should be repeated after every meal, at frequent intervals during the day, early every morning, and last thing at night. A week or so of this régime and house training is well on the way to being achieved.

The same routine, with obvious modifications, can be used for an older dog which may come from a kennel where no house training is done.

Any other formal training can be left until the puppy is three or four months old. But even the youngest puppy will soon realize what the word 'no' means, uttered with some emphasis and repeated if necessary. No opportunity should be lost in starting this very simple form of training.

All puppies should be trained to be left alone at times. The dog which howls or whines persistently when left is a difficult problem. Dalmatians love to be with their owners, but if in early days a puppy is trained to remain alone, beginning with very short periods, the lesson will soon be learned and will be of great use throughout the dog's life.

No attention should be paid to whimpering or whining, hard-hearted as this may seem, and the owner should not return until the puppy is quiet, as it must not be allowed to believe that its complaints have succeeded. As soon as noise stops, the owner can go in and praise the puppy, perhaps giving it a titbit, but always making clear that it is a good dog and he is pleased with it.

Many such minor trials of strength are involved in training the young Dalmatian and they must be won by the owner, not by force, but by the puppy's own acceptance and obedience.

CAR TRAINING

Most Dalmatians enjoy travelling by car and puppies must be introduced to it in early life. The first journeys should be very short, prefaced if possible by allowing the pup to sit in the car with its owner for a few minutes before starting the engine.

Most puppies vomit once or twice during the early stages of training, but get over it very quickly. I found that the easiest way of persuading a puppy that car journeys are something to look forward to, was to introduce a walk, even if only a short one, into every journey. This is easy in the country, and towns have their parks and open spaces. This method is extremely successful. The association of car and walk persists for the dog's entire lifetime.

Should long journeys be necessary before a youngster is fully car trained, those to distant shows for instance, the veterinary surgeon should be asked for a sedative. These should not be needed for long.

It is inadvisable to give a meal before a journey by car, but a tablespoonful of glucose dissolved in water is useful.

A psychological factor may be involved in this matter, for I have never known even a part-trained puppy to be sick on the homeward journey, though it is difficult to imagine that the dog is able to distinguish between the two.

LEAD TRAINING

All dogs should be taught to walk quietly on a lead, not only for the convenience of the owner, but because of the need for its use on the roads of today. The loose dog, even if trained to some extent, must be a danger to itself and other road users and sudden emergencies can always arise.

A collar can be introduced to the puppy after eight weeks or so; it should never be left on when puppies are playing together or it will inevitably be chewed. It will be accepted very quickly, probably after several attempts to scratch it off.

The next step is to attach a long lead, or preferably a long cord, to the collar, and let the pup become used to loss of complete freedom. So far it has come and gone as it pleased, now it must learn restraint.

The pup may resent this at the first attempt. It should be allowed to go some distance, and then stopped and called back, coaxed if necessary with a titbit. The reaction to a call when the puppy has been used to handling and petting is to return, and it must then be praised. Should it refuse after a slight pull on the cord another attempt must be made. If necessary the owner should go to the puppy, taking in the cord as he goes, pick it up, and start again. It is a mistake to drag the puppy back. If the pup is always praised and given a titbit when it returns to a call, even if not very promptly, this lesson will be learned quickly. A whistle can be used as an alternative.

A lead can soon be substituted for the long line and the puppy introduced to walking on the road with its owner. The lead should not be unduly long, it is best held in the right hand and the puppy on the left, away from the on-coming traffic.

The left hand should control the dog by holding the lead near the collar, or as near as possible in the case of a puppy, which should be encouraged to walk along with its owner, even if only for a very short distance. Lessons must of course be very short and the puppy must not become bored.

Preliminary lessons should take place at home and no distractions should be allowed. Puppies must always be taught singly, with nothing to take their attention from the lesson. Pulling should be firmly discouraged. Once a youngster has been allowed to pull steadily against its collar it is extremely difficult to check this and a lifetime of pulling may result. A sharp twitch on the lead, with the command 'back', should stop this habit. It is fatal to pull against the dog. Choke collars are often used in lead training, but ought not to be needed. A tap on the nose from a rolled-up newspaper is often recommended and can be tried if necessary.

The pace should be moderate, neither too fast nor too slow, for no dog likes a slow walking pace and the more natural the pace the more likely the dog is to adopt it.

When success has been achieved, even if only for a short distance, the puppy should be praised effusively and the lesson may be suspended for the time being.

Patience is the quality most demanded of the trainer of a puppy. Impatience or loss of temper may undo the work of weeks.

COMING TO A CALL OR A WHISTLE
There are many occasions when it is imperative that a dog should come to a call, and this lesson should be instilled early in life. The Dalmatian puppy's natural instinct is to run

to its owner and this should always be encouraged. Names should be given to puppies during the first weeks of life, and these should always be used in calling, with praise when the puppy responds. This habit will remain and a call or a whistle will bring the adult dog at a run.

Dalmatians which get plenty of free exercise in country areas often go far afield, though they always know where their owner is. But there may be occasions when they are too far afield for a normal whistle to reach them. In this case the 'Acme' silent whistle is most useful. This has a note (which can be varied) so high-pitched as to be inaudible to the human ear. I have found this signal instantly obeyed by my Dalmatians wherever they may be. I used it seldom, and the dogs understood it to mean urgency and never failed to respond.

The fact that Dalmatians hate above all things to lose their owners probably has something to do with their readiness to come to call or whistle.

In any form of training a command once given must be obeyed, however long it may take. Puppies are quick to learn, as spoiled children are, that they can avoid doing something they do not want to do by wearing down their owner's patience, and this lesson, like more useful ones, is never forgotten once the puppy has been allowed to learn it. No command therefore should be given unless it can be enforced.

The following hints may be found useful to novice owners.

Never give a command which the Dalmatian is unlikely to obey unless you have the power and the patience to enforce it.

Never call or whistle a dog unless it can be expected to come.

Never shout at your dog except in case of emergency. The dog which is constantly shouted at takes no notice of anything else.

Never scold or punish a dog which returns to your call, even if tardily. The dog's mind associates every action with what has immediately preceded it and will therefore consider itself punished, not for running away, but for returning.

In dealing with smaller breeds obedience can be achieved by physical force, a small dog can be lifted from a chair if it refuses to get down. But these methods are impossible with dogs of Dalmatian size. Obedienc involves action on the dog's part. Therefore be sparing in commands, and never allow the dog to realize that it has the power to defy you.

The Dalmatian's desire to please and its affectionate nature and love of approval do much to make training easy and pleasant for both dog and owner.

8
Shows and Showing

Among the many breeds which adorn the show-ring today the Spotted Dog is one of the most spectacular. Harmoniously built, with no structural exaggerations, alert and strikingly decorated, a ring full of Dalmatians is something to rejoice the heart of any lover of an unspoiled and ancient breed.

The Dalmatian takes well to showing. He is something of an extrovert and is easily taught to make the best of himself. Some need little or no training, they are natural showmen. They move easily and well, and themselves adopt a natural stance which shows off their elegant shape to perfection.

Such natural showmanship is a great advantage in the show-ring. Though not in the majority, there are usually a few such dogs in every generation and they are long remembered.

Dalmatians present none of the problems which beset many breeds. Not for them the plucking, the hairdressing, the chalk, the ever-twitching brush. They need no pushing and pulling into position and none of the overhandling so common and often so ludicrous in some breeds.

All dogs need good food, plenty of excercise, and regular grooming. These, with ring-training and a bath before a show, are all the show preparations a Dalmatian needs. Moreover it is an 'honest' breed in which faults of conformation cannot be concealed by the frills and furbelows of an exuberant coat.

Dalmatian owners are not always interested in showing. Many own these dogs because they are such satisfactory companions. But quite often a pet owner finds that his puppy has grown into a good specimen of its breed. Perhaps this owner has a natural eye for a dog (probably the best endowment any fairy godmother could bestow on a godchild destined to feel that life is not complete without one). It is not always easy for a breeder to be certain how a puppy will turn out. Not all apparent starlets fulfil their early promise: the ugly duckling may undergo its traditional transformation. A good dog will, in the end, be recognized by somebody, even if not by its owner, and the advice will be given 'you ought to show him'. Or perhaps the owner, blessed with an enquiring mind (another gift of life-long value), may decide to go to a show and see for himself whether or not his pet suffers by comparison with the dogs he sees in the ring. At the moment he decides that it does not suffer, the future exhibitor is born, or, as some would have it, an incurable disease has been contracted. This may fluctuate, it may have its relapses and recoveries; age, infirmity, and other circumstances may cause showing to be suspended or even abandoned, but with regret and nostalgia. Love of a chosen breed lasts for a lifetime.

It is remarkable how many prominent Dalmatian breeders started their careers in this way almost by accident. These are the people who stay longest in the breed, who are not discouraged by initial lack of success nor spoiled by success when it comes. They put more into the breed than they take out and we are fortunate in having a number of them.

'An eye for a dog'; how often this phrase is heard! My own view is that this faculty is part of a general capacity to appreciate balance and proportions, a harmonious relation between the several parts so that the whole gives a feeling of 'rightness' and entirely satisfies the eye. This 'eye' can be applied in many directions, to architecture, to decoration, to furniture, even to clothes. It can be cultivated to some extent in dogs, and the essential is to own and constantly to observe a well-made dog. Its anatomy must be correct, even if it fails in such breed points as spotting. This can be assessed by anyone. It is a fact that the eye quickly becomes accustomed to anything it has constantly before it, and finally accepts it as normal. Any departure from this normal offends the eye and seems 'wrong'. Hence the supreme important of having a well-balanced and correctly proportioned animal as a pattern.

I would therefore advise any novice with a leaning towards showing to be careful in his first choice of a Dalmatian. If he is not able instinctively to assess balance and proportions, he should get someone who has this gift to help in the choice.

But we must now be practical and tell the would-be exhibitor exactly how to set about showing his first Dalmatian.

Registration by the Kennel Club is the first step, for no unregistered dog may be shown at any show recognized by and under the control of the Kennel Club.

A puppy bought from a breeder may be already registered, and in this case the breeder should hand over the registration certificate, the pedigree, and a transfer form to the new owner when the transaction is completed. If the dog is not registered the owner may apply to the Kennel Club, 1–4 Clarges Street, Piccadilly, London, W1Y 8AB, for a form which he should read carefully and complete in exact accordance with instructions. The breeder's signature to 'the Breeder's Declaration' must be signed and the parents must be registered for the dog to be entered in the Class 1 register. In line with almost everything else Kennel Club Fees have increased and are now as follows: Charge to register a litter is £5 with £1 for each puppy if un-named. If the breeder wishes to name the puppies the initial charge is £5 with an additional £5 for each puppy. The cost of a transfer to a new owner is also £5.

Transfer is the next step to showing if a registered puppy is concerned. It marks the official change of ownership as far as the Kennel Club is concerned; transfer or the lack of it does not affect legal ownership. The new owner should make sure that the breeder has completed his part of the transfer form, fill in his own, and send it to the Kennel Club with the fee.

Should he wish to enter a dog at a show before the official certificates of registration and/or transfer have come through, he may do so by writing NAF or TAF after the dog's name on the show entry form. The signify Name applied for, and Transfer applied for, respectively.

THE NOVICE DOG

Training to the show-ring is the first step to success and it is often ignored by the novice owner with disastrous results. The simple lessons to be learned before the dog goes into the ring are easily absorbed. They will be dealt with in detail, but first, reasons for them should be mentioned. The judge cannot assess the merits of a dog unless he can see it moving naturally, standing normally, and allowing him to handle it. A dog so boisterous that it never has more than two feet on the ground at the same time, or so scared that it tucks itself up, drops its tail between its legs, and hangs its head dismally, shows no sign of its real merit and is impossible to judge.

Another and most important reason for teaching ring behaviour to the youngster is this: the boldest puppy may be wary in new and unfamiliar surroundings. A less tough animal may be frightened, especially if a country dog unused to big buildings, crowds, and the assorted noises met with at any big show. Dogs are creatures of habit, and an action repeated half a dozen times becomes a habit with the greatest ease. On entering a ring, the show-trained puppy quickly recognizes the routine; surroundings may be different but the drill is the same, and the trained puppy carries out its familiar task with confidence. It is only fair and kind to any dog to give it the best chance both of winning a prize and of realizing that a show is nothing to be afraid of.

A prospective showdog should be taken about and accustomed to people and traffic and should be handled by as many people as possible during the course of its training. A few minutes daily devoted to practice and the lessons to be mentioned shortly will be enough. After a week or two they will be absorbed and my experience is that once learned they are never forgotten even after a prolonged absence from the ring. Three minutes practice as a refresher course and the dog will carry out the drill perfectly.

The teacher must remember that infinite patience is

needed and the dog must understand what he is required to do. Gentleness and consistence are other necessary qualities, and the teacher must never never lose his temper. Puppies are volatile creatures with butterfly minds, and many minutes of concentration are almost impossible. Lessons must be short. Dalmatians are sensitive dogs and respond best to a gentle manner and a quiet voice. Punishments are quite out of place here; rewards on the contrary are useful crutches. They should be accompanied by a pat and a word of praise. Show training must not become a game, though a romp and a run may well precede it. Once the show-lead is on, the puppy must give his attention to the job. Hence the need for very short lessons, for the pupil must never be bored.

Show training can begin as soon as the puppy is accustomed to collar and lead and at least by the age of six months.

Difficult Dogs. There are some Dalmatians, as there are dogs of every breed, which do not respond to training. Among them are the fundamentally nervous animals to which shows seem a nightmare of fear. These are uncommon among Dalmatians and are not typical of the breed. Unless this condition of abnormal nervousness is due to some unfortunate experience, which in time may be forgotten, these dogs will never do any good in the show-ring, as indeed they should not, for the condition is often hereditary, and in the interests of the breed no such dog should be allowed to pass on the tendency. Moreover to force such dogs to undergo the terrifying experience a show would appear to be for them, is hardly less than cruelty.

The excessively boisterous dog is also a problem though a far less serious one. Maturity sobers most Dalmatians, and these often become excellent showmen, their old exuberance calmed to an interested awareness which is an asset in the show-ring.

The third class of difficult dog is also rare, but it is known to most exhibitors. It is the dog, often excellent in appearance and behaviour at home, which becomes completely bored in the ring. To rouse it from this gloomy state is often impossible, and a ringsider might well imagine the dog to be ill-treated, so glum and apathetic does it appear. It hates a show, though once away it often becomes a different animal altogether. If a little experience does not correct this behaviour such a dog is better left at home.

Every dog should learn the following lessons before it appears in the show-ring for the first time. It is only too obvious, unfortunately, that many novices do not recognize the importance of pre-show training.

1. To walk and trot in a string of dogs at a steady pace round the ring without pulling out, in both an anti-clockwise and clockwise direction. The dog is normally led on the left side of the handler, anti-clockwise, but when moving in the opposite clockwise direction the dog is led on the right, and the Dalmatian must be trained to go equally well on this side.

Every dog has its own best pace, at which it moves most easily. The owner cannot see this when moving his own dog. Too slow a rate is unnatural to the Dalmatian; few, if any, proceed at a slow walk. This may cause the dog to pace. Too fast a rate is apt to break into a canter. A knowledgeable friend is needed to watch this exercise and give his opinion on the best rate for the individual dog, he can also move the dog himself for the owner to observe its gait.

2. To stand quietly in a good position to be looked over by the judge and afterwards handled. Normally the judge calls dog and owner to the centre of the ring for this. He will want to see the dog's 'bite', that is the relative position of the front teeth which should be in accordance with the standard, namely a scissor bite. The owner should show the teeth himself and should accustom the dog from puppy-hood onwards to allow this to be done. By gently lifting the upper lip with one hand and pushing the lower lip down with the other, the teeth are seen easily and quickly.

3. To move across the ring away from the back towards the judge in a straight line at a steady pace. To do this the handler must watch the judge and not the dog, or he will find himself well away from the proper course. This exercise enables the judge to assess fore and hind action. Most judges

like a side view of the animal in addition, which shows the
length of stride and the propulsive power of the quarters.

The dog should be handled throughout on a fairly slack
lead. Many have their heads and necks stretched up tightly.
The object of this is often to disguise loose skin round the
throat or perhaps upright shoulders. Both are faults. Any
dog can be trained to move on a slack lead so that its natural
action can be seen and this is what the judge wants, and
sometimes insists on seeing.

An artificially produced pose, a normally drooping tail
held in position, or a sagging head supported, hides, or may
hide, defects of structure or temperament. Many novices
use these methods because they imagine them to be correct
and for no other reason, but they must not blame the judge
if he wonders what they are trying to hide.

Dalmatians are exceptionally easy to train to show themselves well, and every novice exhibitor ought to make a
point of this preliminary training. Many bring completely
untrained dogs into the ring and are surprised, sometimes
indignant, that they do not win. I must stress that the show-
ring itself is no place for training.

How early should a puppy be shown. The earliest age at which a
puppy may be shown is six months. Many exhibitors start
their puppies' show careers at this age. Six-month-old
Dalmatian puppies are immature and, in competition with
puppies of eleven to twelve months of age, are giving away
far too much. I believe it to be wiser to wait until the
youngster is at least eight months old or even nine months,
when it will suffer less in comparison with more mature
animals. This is especially important in the case of a first-
class puppy. To have it put down on the score of immaturity
may handicap its progress. Memories are short and while the
fact that it was put down will be remembered, the reason
may well be forgotten.

It is unwise to over-show any dog and especially a puppy.
A taste of boredom and staleness may easily develop in a
youngster taken too often to shows. This may take a long
time to cure. Moreover the young animal cannot have its

routine of rest, exercise, and feeding constantly interrupted without suffering in its development both physical and mental.

The Junior Warrant has sometimes been blamed for over-showing of young stock. This is an award instituted by the Kennel Club shortly before the Second World War. It is won by a dog under eighteen months of age, which has won twenty-five points, acquired at shows as follows. First Prize at any championship shows where challenge certificates are offered for the breed scores three points. First Prize at open shows scores one point. It is true that youngsters are occasionally taken from show to show in the pursuit of this award. This unwise procedure is not common among Dalmatian exhibitors.

A first-class dog, even starting its show career at the age of nine months, usually has no difficulty in gaining the Junior Warrant, but over-showing undoubtedly defeats its own ends, resulting in boredom and staleness which may never be overcome, quite apart from the effects which constant interruptions of the regular life may have on the dog. It is wrong and most unwise to pursue the Junior Warrant at the expense of the young dog's future.

To the Novice Exhibitor. Attend a few shows before launching your dog on a show career. You will see examples of good ring behaviour on the part of both exhibitor and dog (and possibly the reverse). The good handler is usually the person who appears to be leaving it all to the dog. Either he has a born showman or he is a good trainer.

Write to the show secretary for a schedule of any show you wish to attend. All shows are advertised in the canine press (*Our Dogs* and *Dog World*). Fill the entry form in carefully after reading it with attention and post it on or before the date on which entries close.

Prepare everything you will need for the show in advance. A bench rug for your dog's comfort and to keep it clean; a bench chain and collar, a suitable lead for the ring, and the less obtrusive this is the better. A thin white buckskin slip-lead hardly shows on the dog and can be loosened to lie round the neck to give a more natural line. A drinking bowl should be taken, for water is always available at shows; milk is appreciated by some Dalmatians.

A brush for final sprucing and a damp chamois leather to remove travel stains is advisable. It should be an unbroken rule that the dog starts from home clean. Titbits for the ring should also be small, boiled liver in small pieces is perhaps the best, it should never be thrown down in the ring. Vetzyme tablets are just as appetizing to most dogs. Although many exhibitors take the dog's normal midday meal, I have never done so. No well-fed dog is harmed by missing a meal, which in any case should not be given before the dog has been finally judged. A few dry biscuits will meet the case if food is required.

A show bag, and it should be capacious, is necessary to carry show gear, with bench rug, towel, and perhaps the owner's personal possessions, and exhibitors should never leave money or valuables about at an unattended bench. Anyone can attend a show by paying for admission, and crooks have become aware of this and often make substantial hauls from careless or too trustful exhibitors.

Never take a bitch in season to a show, especially a show in which other breeds follow Dalmatians into the ring. A bitch in full season, meeting a dog either at the entrance where the animals are perforce herded together, or in the next bench, can so upset it as to make it impossible to show.

To say the least of it, this is an unsporting action and likely to reduce considerably the exhibitor's popularity.

Get to the show in good time, a flustered exhibitor usually means a flustered dog, neither are at their best. Watch for your first class, and shortly before it is likely to begin give your dog a run or walk round to loosen it up.

Remember that there is more to showing than holding a lead with a dog attached to the other end. Concentration is the first essential for the handler. Your dog and the judge should be your only concern.

Handle your dog as little as possible. It is easy to show a Dalmatian without even touching it in the ring. Should the dog be standing awkwardly, turn it round quietly still on a slack lead and bring it up again.

Your dog can relax when the judge is concentrating on another exhibit, but you should be ready to alert it at any moment for the judge may glance in your direction for purposes of comparison. A dog caught on the wrong foot may lose a prize it might otherwise have won, but do not keep your dog rigidly at attention throughout, there are obvious opportunities for allowing it to relax.

Do not chat with ringsiders or other exhibitors when in the ring, concentrate entirely on the dog.

Encourage your dog to use its ears and tail by talking to it quietly. Titbits can also be used for this; even the rustle of paper in a pocket will produce the desired result in a trained dog.

In a sloping ring always keep your dog facing uphill. Facing downhill spoils the top line making the rump appear higher than the shoulders.

Always keep your dog between yourself and the judge.

Never speak to the judge unless he asks you a question. If he does, answer it briefly and do not volunteer information.

Remember that a gloating winner is as unpleasant as a bad loser. Sour and unfriendly looks from a loser are noticed by the ringsiders and will be duly marked to the discredit of the person concerned.

Contrary to popular impressions, the normal Dalmatian does not dislike shows. It does not resent being attached to its little cubicle of a bench, it regards this as its temporary lodging, and the sympathy of the average onlooker is quite wasted. The appearance of a show bag the night before a show is greeted with enthusiasm and excitement and the gloom of any dogs left behind the next morning is only too obvious.

If you are showing a bitch do not be unduly anxious if she refuses to relieve herself during an entire day, especially if the show is indoors. I have never known any of my bitches make use of the space provided and they have been neither uncomfortable nor injured in any way. But a good run before a show should always be given if at all possible.

You will meet with immense friendliness among Dalmatian enthusiasts, help and advice will be freely given. It is better, however, not to ask for this from an exhibitor who has only just arrived and is busy benching his dog, nor from one just about to to into the ring. Plenty of other opportunities will arise during the course of the show.

Remember always that there is a lot to learn; your job as a novice is to find out what makes a good Dalmatian, and to recognize it when you see it. You have also to learn to recognize faults in your own dog. It is always easy to do so in those of other people.

Remember too that there are ungenerous people in every breed; even though few, the harm they may do is out of proportion to their numbers. Severe, perhaps unwarranted, criticism may mean merely that you have a dog which could be a rival to one owned by the critic. This may be, in a backhanded way, a compliment. Few people waste their time in running down a bad dog.

And finally remember once more that there is a lot to learn before anyone can consider himself an expert, and there are some things which only experience can teach.

9
Breeding and Puppy Rearing

The Dalmatian enthusiast will not long remain content with showing, absorbing and exciting as this is. He will certainly wish to breed for himself and will look forward to his home-bred puppies and to the pleasure of showing them and of establishing a strain of his own by careful breeding.

To begin such a career by buying one or two bitch puppies, rearing them to maturity, showing them, and then breeding from them, is most satisfying, besides ensuring that the novice has gained a certain amount of knowledge and experience before embarking on a pursuit which needs both to be successful.

There is another shorter method; this is to acquire an adult bitch on 'breeding terms'. The bitch is loaned from her owner to the second party to the agreement for a specified period, usually until she has had a litter. She then normally becomes the property of the borrower as soon as the provisions of the agreement have been fulfilled, usually the handing over, unregistered, of a puppy or puppies from the litter.

The method may be a lucrative source of income to an astute breeder who may have a number of bitches out on breeding terms from which will be acquired free, or practically free, a number of puppies which can be immediately sold without the seller having been involved in any sort of expense. No verbal arrangement on breeding terms should ever be agreed to, the possibilities of friction between the parties are too great. The Kennel Club will provide a form on which the provisions are specified, such items as who should pay the stud fee, or any veterinary expenses incurred, at what age and by whom the puppy or puppies should be chosen, the position if only one puppy is born,

115

and so on. This is signed by both parties and sent to the Kennel Club, who will register it and the possibilities of disputes are greatly reduced thereby.

It is not possible within the limits of this book to go fully into the principles of breeding, nor to describe the practical side of whelping and all that this involves in the fullest detail. The reader is referred to the author's *Practical Dog Breeding and Genetics* which is entirely devoted to the subject.

Briefly there are three main breeding systems, two of which are similar in principle and are based on relationship between the partners. These are In-breeding and Line-breeding. The third, Out-breeding, is, as its name implies, based on the absence of any relationship as far as possible. As systems go, this amounts to random breeding, in that the relationship between the animals is neither greater nor less than would be expected at any random mating.

In-breeding may be considered as mating individuals of the closest possible relationship, father-daughter, mother-son, brother-sister, though a rather wider interpretation is usual; the essence is that relationship must be close. This system cannot introduce anything new into the hereditary pattern, it can only reproduce factors already present in the parents and possibly fix them. It can also bring to light factors hitherto unsuspected. It is therefore a useful means of fixing good points and disclosing bad, making it possible to eliminate the latter by breeding them out.

In-breeding is good or bad only in so far as the inheritance of the animals concerned is good or bad. It is two-edged, and not a method for the novice breeder. Bad points are fixed just as surely as good and unless the forbears are known to the breeder, not only as names on pedigrees, but as individuals with all their characteristics, in-breeding may be disastrous. In any case the first generation is not a true test; for its effect to be seen in-breeding must be continued for several generations, and each must be accompanied by strict culling. Stock used for in-breeding must be exceptionally good and must be free from serious faults, above all, any faults common to both parents.

Line-breeding is a modified form of in-breeding, neither as rapid in its results nor as liable to catastrophe. It consists of breeding within a related family, or strain (the essence of a strain as the word is used in breeding, is relationship between the animals concerned).

If general all-round improvement in stock is desired, then close breeding with the necessary culling will give the best results. If an occasional outstanding animal is wanted without reference to general quality, out-crossing is as likely to produce it as any other method. But the good qualities of such an animal are less likely to be transmitted to its progeny because they are less likely to be possessed in duplicate, and therefore passed on to every puppy.

We turn now to the practical side of breeding, and to the management of the stud dog and the brood bitch.

The Stud Dog should be in the pink of condition, well fed on a high protein diet, well exercised, lean, and hard. Stud dogs and bitches in season should be kept apart, preferably out of sight and sound of each other, for the scent of a bitch in season is a powerful stimulus to the dog's mating instinct, and if frustrated he loses condition rapidly, often entirely refusing food. If a pair live together the bitch should be removed when her heat begins, for one cannot tell just when the dog will become interested in her scent, it may not be for the first week, it may be earlier, but once this has occurred the damage is done as far as he is concerned, and a dog subjected to frequent frustrated stimulation of this kind often endures real misery which is detrimental to his health and may interfere with his function.

A stud dog should not be reproved for his attention to bitches in season, it is normal and natural and the remedy is to keep them apart. Unfortunately dogs are at the mercy of the careless pet owners who often allow in-season bitches to roam the streets and make the lives of dogs miserable by their scent. There is only one way of saving dogs from this, and ensuring that bitches are not molested during their heat, and this is to keep bitches in season strictly isolated and enclosed within a fence which no dog can penetrate or climb, with, if possible, a no-man's-land between them and any stud dog in the Kennel.

THE BROOD BITCH

It is equally important for the brood bitch to be healthy and hard, well fed, and well exercised. A fat bitch is less likely to conceive and may have more trouble in whelping. When bitches only are kept she may lead her normal life, though if she can be kept off roads and public places altogether her owner is spared trouble from dogs which have caught her scent. She should in any case never be allowed out except on collar and lead. Even a small garden, if securely fenced, will be enough for health and restricted exercise for three weeks twice yearly. In any breeding kennel a separate building is normally provided for bitches in season away from all dogs, and to prevent loneliness I always used to put two together even if the second were not in season. A bitch to be mated should not be allowed with the dog until she is believed to be ready for mating, and should be returned to her seclusion afterwards for the remainder of the period. She will still be attractive to dogs for several days and may herself be eager for a repetition of the experience.

The Bitch in Season. The first heat in Dalmatian bitches usually occurs at any time between about eight months and a year, sometimes earlier, sometimes later. Dalmatians, like other breeds of roughly the same size, do not mature as early as do the smaller breeds, and it is unwise to mate at the first season, unless it is delayed until the second year of life. A bitch is normally a puppy when she has her first heat, her own frame is not fully developed and the production of a litter is likely to interfere with her own development or with the nutrition of her offspring.

The season, or oestrus as it is technically called, is roughly divided into three stages, each occupying about a week. During the first week the uterus is being prepared by a reproductive hormone for the reception of the fertilized eggs, and this is indicated by a slight vaginal discharge, at first almost colourless, but becoming more profuse and blood-stained, accompanied by an enlargement and hardening of the vulva.

During the second week the discharge increases and has the appearance of blood and is usually at its maximum about the middle of this period. Towards the end of the second week the discharge is lessening, becoming paler and less staining, and the vulva is softening and becoming loose and flaccid.

It is at this stage that mating becomes possible, and the bitch normally will not accept the dog until it has been reached. The ovary will be shedding its eggs and a mating is not fruitful except at this time. Normally the time for mating is reached from about the eleventh day onwards for three, four, or even five days; it may be somewhat earlier or considerably later, even in a normal healthy bitch.

Breeders must abandon the idea of a 'right' day for mating. This varies not only from bitch to bitch but from one heat to another in the same bitch. The right day is that on which the eggs begin to be shed from the ovary, and this the normal bitch will indicate in no uncertain manner in the presence of a dog, or of another bitch, if an attempt is made to mount her. This often happens between bitches when one is in season.

The response is for the tail to be switched aside and held rigidly, and for the bitch to brace herself to receive a possible mate, with signs of sexual excitement.

I have found it good practice to mate a bitch twenty-four hours after she will first stand to the dog, and have never mated twice provided the first mating has been satisfactory, that is, the bitch willing, the mating entirely unforced, and the tie of normal length, from fifteen minutes upwards. This presupposes animals of normal sexual behaviour and Dalmatians have lost none of their natural instincts. They are good breeders, easy whelpers, and excellent mothers. The infertility which afflicts some breeds does not affect our own. Frigidity and infertility are likely to be due to abnormalities or defects in the system of reproductive hormones which controls the entire breeding cycle. Such conditions are likely to be due to hereditary causes, and it would be foolish to attempt to breed from such animals, even if it were possible. Fertility is the necessity of any breed, progressively reduced fertility will cause affected breeds to decline and eventually to disappear.

Mating is a natural event and no difficulty is likely to occur in Dalmatians with a virile dog and a bitch of normal instincts. The pair should be introduced to each other, and as soon as it is seen that they are friendly, they should be allowed a period of courtship, in which the dog makes advances; the bitch behaves with a certain coyness and show of resistance, but after a short time the pair understand each other and mating is achieved easily.

The bitch should wear a collar so that she can be restrained if necessary and she should be steadied when the dog mounts her as she may easily pull away at a first mating. During the mating it is wise to control the pair by staying at the head of the bitch. A camp-stool is a convenience at this stage.

When the dog is ready to turn, after five minutes or so of contact, he may be helped by lifting one foreleg over the bitch's back so that both forelegs are on the same side of her, followed by lifting over the hind leg of the same side; the pair are then standing comfortably back to back. When they separate, and no attempt to hurry this should be made, the bitch should be taken back to her kennel, and the dog to his own place.

Formerly the bitch used always to be taken to the dog. Nowadays it is quite usual for the owner of the dog to be willing to take him to the bitch, and this may be a convenience. The bitch's owner should of course be prepared to pay the expenses of the visit together with the stud fee, at the time of service. This fee is for the use of the dog, it does not depend on the result of the mating, and if the bitch has no puppies, the owner has no claim against the owner of the stud dog. However, it is customary to give a second service to the same bitch if she misses, and this should be arranged at the time of the first service.

Other arrangements are often made, such as one or two puppies from the litter as substitute for a stud fee. The novice owner may be glad to have fewer puppies to sell, but as the terms normally include the pick of the litter, and perhaps also a second choice, the breeder may regret the arrangement.

He would be wise to pay the stud fee and have a free hand over the litter.

It is not uncommon for forced matings to take place, either because the breeder is in a hurry or simply from ignorance of the psychological and physiological factors involved in the animals concerned. Animals are not machines and forced matings are rape. Moreover they are not very likely to be successful.

There are dogs, and bitches, which will mate with one partner and not with another, and these preferences should be respected.

The Bitch in Whelp. Little change in appearance will be noticed for several weeks of pregnancy though a slight filling in of the flanks may be seen if the litter is the large one so normal in Dalmatians. By five weeks the condition should be obvious and it is often clear much sooner.

Feeding should be as usual during the first month but protein is the constituent of food most needed during pregnancy because it provides body-building material, and up to twelve or even more small bodies have to be made during the short period of nine weeks. Some of the bitch's starchy foods should therefore be replaced with extra meat, fish, eggs, cheese, and other animal products. Liver in small amounts is especially useful.

Additional minerals are advisable, so that the bitch does not deplete her own supplies, for a shortage of lime (calcium) is likely to result in eclampsia towards the end of the nursing period. The animal body needs lime and phosphorus in a certain ratio, together with Vitamin D for their assimilation and utilization. These are needed for the laying down of bone in the puppy skeleton and some preparation containing them is useful during pregnancy and lactation.

Stress, made by Phillips Yeast Products, is a useful balanced mineral supplement, which, with one drop of halibut-liver oil daily for Vitamin D, will supply all the minerals needed. A preparation for human use including Vitamin D, called Ostocalcium (Glaxo), is another excellent product.

Exercise is important. It keeps the muscles in tone for the

work they have to do in stimulating circulation and the elimination of waste products from the bowel, and eventually in expelling the puppies. The in-whelp bitch should not be treated as an invalid, though during the later weeks she should not be allowed rough play with other dogs nor should she be overtired in any way. Moderate activity should be encouraged as much as possible and the daily walk is essential, though at her own pace in the last week or two.

During the last week or so of pregnancy movements of the unborn puppies are clearly seen, especially when the bitch is lying quietly on her side.

By this time she will be wanting to make her nest and her whelping place should be ready with bed and bedding. Regular breeders will probably have special heated whelping quarters. A warm kitchen is ideal for the occasional litter and convenient for the breeder, even if the pups go to an outside kennel after a day or two.

Heat is one of the essentials during the first weeks of life. The whelping temperature should not be lower than 75° Fahrenheit. It should remain at this level for two or three days, and, according to the weather, can then be very gradually reduced to normal.

Hardening puppies off is often recommended as a good reason for cold quarters. This process is correct at the proper time, but the proper time is not in the first few weeks. The heat-regulating mechanism of a puppy, like that of a baby, is not fully developed at birth. It is now recognized that babies can die from cold in a normally heated room and puppies are equally susceptible for their normal temperature is higher. Comfortable puppies are quiet and contented, they make better use of their food and grow faster than those reared in cold conditions.

An infra-red lamp, suspended above the whelping box at the distance recommended by the makers, is most satisfactory for heating.

The Whelping Box. The bitch should become used to this by sleeping in it for a week or two before she whelps. It should be large enough to take both bitch and litter with plenty of room and can then be used as a bed for the puppies for the first six or seven weeks.

The whelping box is sometimes covered in, but on the whole an open box makes any handling easier and in a well-heated room the extra warmth given by a cover is not necessary. The sides should be high enough to keep puppies in, but the front should be made with two loose sections, either or both of which can be used, so that puppies can be kept in or allowed to get out. A rail round the three inner sides of the box about three inches from the sides and three or four inches high will serve to protect puppies which may creep behind a bitch during the first few days of life, and get crushed against the sides. Most Dalmatian bitches are very clever at managing their puppies, and will get into a heap of puppies, nudging them neatly aside most carefully, and settling down with them comfortably close to her. A clumsy or agitated bitch can easily cause the death of a puppy if no protection of this sort is provided.

Old woollen rags, blankets, and so on are good material for the actual whelping, anything given will be torn up and arranged to the bitch's liking. All soiled material can be burned when whelping is over.

The fine soft wood shavings known as Wood Wool is excellent for later bedding. The fibres are too soft to cause damage to the puppies and this material is clean, antiseptic, non-absorbent, and warm. It should be relatively easy to obtain.

Whelping. The question of supervision by the breeder is often disputed. Bitches in some breeds may prefer to be left alone. I have never owned a Dalmatian bitch who was not happier when I was with her. Some even would not settle down unless I were there.

Dogs are very quick to sense their owner's moods, and a fussy over-anxious owner may be better away, though the bitch should not be left very long without a visit.

But there is an even better reason for supervision than this. Dalmatians rarely have any difficulties in whelping but occasions do arise when complications occur and the breeder who becomes aware of this in the early stages is in the best position for dealing with them by calling in his veterinary surgeon at once. A few preparations should be ready before whelping starts and the following articles are useful. Sterilized scissors boiled and left in the pan with the water in which they were boiled until they are needed; a solution of Dettol or some other mild antiseptic, cotton-wool pledgets, rough warm towels, a small amount of brandy, and a square of boiled lint or a pair of boiled white cotton gloves. If one wants to identify puppies at birth while they are still wet, a potted-meat jar filled with diluted gentian violet is a good means of doing so, and the pup's tail should be dipped in it. The dye is harmless and fairly lasting and will not easily be licked off by the bitch as it might be if applied to the body surface. Although Dalmatian puppies are born pure white (apart from any with patches) before the bitch has licked them dry, it is sometimes possible to see the skin spotting and this may give a clue to the later pattern. As soon as they are dry they are completely white again and only from about the end of the second week onwards do shadowy spots begin to appear.

The birth of the puppies usually takes place about the sixty-third day from mating but it may be earlier or later by several days. My own experience is that it is quite normal for the bitch to whelp two days early, and I have had one whelp five days early and produce a large litter of perfectly formed healthy puppies. I have found any considerable delay beyond two days to be a danger signal, though many breeders tell me that their bitches go overtime by about a week or more without consequences. This has not been my experience and it is, I believe, prudent to consult the expert in such cases. A visit which the event proves to have been unnecessary is better than a misfortune which a visit could have prevented.

SIGNS OF IMMINENT WHELPING

1. Making a nest, probably a week or rather more before the actual birth.

2. A slight sticky discharge from the vulva, increasing daily. The vulva gradually becomes hard and slightly swollen.

3. A fall in the bitch's temperature (taken in the rectum) of three or four degrees from the normal 101.4°F. and an

increasing discharge. This drop in temperature is a most reliable sign, and any bitch with a normal temperature will not whelp for at least twenty-four hours.

4. Refusal of food, which usually means the onset of labour within a matter of hours. This is usual but not invariable. I had one bitch who was gobbling her supper when the first puppy was born.

5. Restlessness, obvious discomfort, softening and pouting of the vulva with increased discharge. This constitutes the first stage of whelping during which the dilatation of the passages is taking place.

6. Finally the alternate straining with relaxation and panting occurs. This should herald the birth of the first puppy within a short time. The birth passages have been gradually softened and dilated throughout the preceding period to allow the strong expulsive uterine contractions to expel the first puppy. These contractions can be both seen and felt.

The first thing to be seen at the vulva is usually the bag of membranes, filled with fluid and acting to dilate the passages as well as to protect the whelp from pressure. This bag will appear and retreat possibly several times with successive contractions and relaxations but will finally emerge with the puppy inside it, the head downwards and therefore born first. As the head is, at birth, the largest part of the puppy, it will dilate the birth passage so that shoulders and body will usually slip out easily with the next contraction.

A rump-first birth, called 'a breech', is almost as common and usually presents no difficulty, except that the head may be a tight fit, and if the membranes are broken, as they sometimes are, birth must not be delayed or the whelp may suffocate from lack of oxygen.

If the head is near the orifice it can be gently eased out even by an inexperienced breeder, during a contraction, and the boiled square of lint will assist here, for puppies are exceedingly slippery, and it is almost impossible to get a grip with bare fingers. If such a removal is attempted the greatest gentleness and care are needed.

As soon as the pup and placenta are born the bitch will eat

the placenta and bite through the umbilical cord an inch or two from the umbilicus. If she does not eat the placenta the breeder will have to cut the cord with sterilized scissors, first squeezing the blood contained in it along its length to get as much as possible into the puppy's circulation. The cord can be cut and tied with sterilized thread an inch or so from the navel.

If the bitch does not release the puppy from its membranes immediately after birth the breeder must do so himself or it will die of asphyxia. They should be broken gently with the fingers over the region of the mouth so that breathing can begin. This is another good reason for supervising whelping.

As soon as the placenta has disappeared the bitch will lick the puppy dry and during this process will turn it over and over, sometimes even roughly. This should not be prevented, it is the natural instinct to stimulate breathing and establish the independent circulation which begins only at birth. I have never removed puppies after birth. Dalmatians are good mothers and like to fuss over them and are not happy if they are taken away. Just as in mating, bitches have normal instincts in whelping, and can usually safely be allowed to do all that their instinct tells them. The placenta for instance is known to contain a hormone which stimulates milk production.

The interval between the birth of puppies varies considerably, it is quite usual to have two or three in fairly rapid succession and then a long rest of an hour or more before the next emerges. Towards the end of a large litter (and fourteen whelps or even more are quite common), there may be considerable delay between each one. As long as the bitch is resting quietly there is no cause for worry. She may like a drink of warm milk with glucose added and if she seems at all exhausted a teaspoonful of brandy is useful.

When the breeder believes that the last puppy is born, though it is not easy to be perfectly sure of this, the bitch should be taken outside for a few moments, the soiled bedding removed and replaced, either by clean blankets or by the wood wool already mentioned. The bitch can then return to her litter and rest peacefully with the puppies, which should all be feeding.

It is sensible to remove any patched puppies as soon as possible. These should not be kept. A veterinary surgeon will put them down painlessly, but if they are smuggled away as soon as born, immersed and held under in a pail of warm water, the bitch will not miss them and their end will be easy and painless.

The Post-Whelping Period. For a few days after whelping the bitch should have a light milky diet and she seems to prefer it. Meat should be introduced as soon as she will eat. Diarrhoea is quite normal for a few days, with copious black motions, coloured by the blood she has eaten with the placentas. This should clear rapidly; if it is at all persistent doses of charcoal with kaolin are useful. Allen and Hanbury's Charkaolin is excellent and the tasteless granules can be sprinkled on food.

The bitch may be reluctant to leave her puppies for the first day or two, even to relieve herself. In this case a collar and lead will be necessary. As soon as she is ready she can be released to run back to her children.

It is hardly possible to overfeed the nursing bitch if the right kind of food is given. This should be largely protein, meat, fish, cheese, eggs, and milk. She will have a large appetite, as indeed she needs to have, for puppies grow fast and their mother has to supply all material needed for this growth during the first few weeks. She should never be asked to rear too many puppies.

The well-fed puppy will more than double its birth weight by the end of the first week of life, and quadruple it by the third week, making a substantial gain during every succeeding week though the rate becomes progressively less as time goes on. By the time the puppies are being fed by the breeder to any extent, the bitch's food can be gradually reduced until by the time the pups are completely weaned at seven weeks her diet will be back to normal. Adequate mineral supplies with halibut-liver oil should be continued throughout and if the bitch is at all out of condition these supplements may be given for several weeks more. Vetzyme tablets are recommended and one daily should also be given to puppies by the age of five weeks or so, broken into small pieces and mixed with food; they will be eaten greedily.

Weaning. Although weaning as such does not begin until later, puppies should be taught to lap during the third week of life.

Bitches' milk is a great deal richer in fat and protein than cows' milk, which should be modified and enriched if puppies are to be adequately fed in amounts which will not overfill their tiny stomachs. The lesson of learning to lap will not at first provide any substantial addition to their diet, but is useful and could be necessary if for any reason the bitches' milk was insufficient for the litter.

There are many ways of modifying cows' milk; one of the simplest which I used for many years with success is by the addition of full-cream dried milk in the proportions of one heaped tablespoonful to a half pint of cows' milk. The method is to bring the fresh milk rapidly to the boil, stirring to prevent the cream from rising, to cool it slightly, with an occasional stir to prevent a skin forming, and to add it slowly to the dried milk which has been rubbed free from lumps in a dry basin.

This should be fed warm to the puppies; for the first lessons the pup should be held on the lap, and a teaspoonful or two of the mixture put in a saucer and held below the pup's nose. This is often recognized at once and lapping begins. If the pup does not lap, its nose may be gently dipped into the milk. In some cases there may be some preliminary sucking and blowing, but with patience every puppy should have achieved the action of lapping after a single session.

One such feed, increasing the amount slightly every day, can be given for the third week and can be increased to two, still increasing the amount, during the fourth week.

By the time the puppies are four weeks old raw meat should be introduced into the diet with egg yolk into one milk feed daily in the proportion of a single yolk between four pups. Scraped meat is always recommended, and fresh beef is the best, even if it has to be replaced later by other kinds of meat. However, scraping is a long and wearisome process, especially when a large amount has to be prepared,

Ch. Fanhill Faune (*Thomas Fall*)

Ch. Winnall Elegance

Ch. Olbero Onceuponatime (*C.M. Cooke*)

Ch. Horseman's Vogue (*Thomas Fall*)

Scand. Ch. Dallas Super Star (Sweden)

American Ch. Dottidale Jo Jo at 10 years old

Ch. Phaeland Phishpie (*Anne Roslin-Williams*)

Ch. Dapple Dana of Sidlaw

and in practice I have found that raw meat, with all fibrous tissue removed, passed twice through a mincer is perfectly satisfactory and has no ill results of any kind.

One teaspoonful of minced meat per puppy can be given for a few days, increasing the amount gradually. All puppies, without exception in my experience, take greedily to meat. Knackers' meat must not be used without being well cooked.

By this time the pups will be getting less milk from their mother, who during the early days also supplies all the vitamins through her milk. One drop of halibut-liver oil should be included in one feed daily, or if a drop bottle be used, it can be put direct into the pup's mouth, which ensures that every puppy gets its dose.

By the fifth week the puppies should be having one good meat feed and two milk feeds daily, with one egg yolk between four puppies included, with fish as an alternative to meat once or twice weekly.

As the bitches' milk becomes less the amount of the puppies' food must be increased.

It will be noticed that as yet no form of starchy food has been introduced into the diet. Puppies have very small stomachs and, as the main body-building foods are so important during this stage of very rapid growth, a high protein diet is of the greatest importance. After the age of six weeks or so some form of carbohydrate is useful and any cereal with modified milk as before is suitable, though too much should not be given, the mainstay should still be protein. Farex is useful as the first cereal.

By this time the bitch will probably be vomiting her half-digested food for the puppies. This is a natural procedure, a sign that a mixed diet is now needed, and should not be interfered with, except to ensure that no unsuitable food is given to the bitch.

The entire weaning process should be a gradual one and the puppies should gain weight steadily throughout. The change-over from maternal feeding to independent meals should be so well managed that the pups thrive and the bitch returns to normal by the end of the period.

At *seven weeks* meals can be as follows:

8–9 a.m. Modified milk with Farex or other cereal and egg yolk, about a quarter pint to each puppy.

11–12 noon. Raw meat cut small, or broken-up fish, with an equal amount of brown bread or wholemeal biscuit meal, soaked but not sloppy with bone broth or weak marmite. One drop of halibut-liver oil and one crushed Vetzyme tablet to each puppy.

2 p.m. A visit from the bitch. She will probably vomit food for the pups. If she has no milk a drink of modified milk should be given.

5 p.m. A good feed of modified milk as at 8. a.m. but without egg.

8 p.m. A good feed or raw meat, cut small. Mincing can be given up at this age, for dogs do not chew their food. Their stomachs are constructed to deal with solid lumps of meat, and though these should not be too big for puppies of this age, it is a mistake to continue too long with meat minced or cut too small.

The amount of every feed should be as much as the puppy will eat greedily. The differ very much in their requirements and this test is fairly reliable as a guide, for it is impossible to give exact amounts. A puppy of seven weeks should be having about six ounces of meat daily.

A large marrow bone sawn in sections, but not chopped because of splintering, is not only a source of nourishment because of the marrow which will be licked out, but a plaything which will amuse the puppies for hours, and they will not be able to chew fragments of this particularly solid bone.

After the age of seven weeks the bitch is unlikely to have milk for her puppies and they should not be allowed to worry her if she resents it. This will be quite obvious.

She will not want to sleep with them, but should be allowed with them during the day when she wishes, and she will enjoy playing with them.

Feeding of puppies should be continued on the same lines and amounts should be increased fairly rapidly to match their appetites. A steady regular gain in weight is essential, for growth is rapid still, and the foundations of future health and good constitution are laid during the first year of life.

Any early set-backs may be difficult to put right. The wise breeder sees to it that puppies are fed and managed so that progress is uninterrupted.

And as far as feeding goes, we now leave our eight-week-old puppies, to return to other details of early management from birth onwards.

PUPPY MANAGEMENT IN EARLY LIFE
During the first two or three weeks of life the puppies can safely be left to the management of the bitch except for a few particular events. Dalmatians are exceptionally good mothers and easy to manage at this period. Although devoted to their children, bitches which trust their owners will allow their puppies to be handled freely from birth onwards. It is better, however, not to allow strangers to visit bitch and litter for at least the first week and only then if the bitch makes no objection. Some bitches resent the presence of other dogs during the early days, but not all do so and I have had those which welcome a friendly bitch as a sort of nanny, to help in the grooming and clearing-up operations, but this is, I think, rather unusual.

Dew Claws. Although I have never seen a Dalmatian with dew claws on its hind legs, they are always present on the forelegs and should be removed, for they serve no useful purpose, in fact they are a nuisance in several ways – the idea that removing them weakens the legs is one of those old wives' tales best forgotten like many others. If they are left, they must be trimmed from time to time throughout life, or they grow so long that they may curl round into the legs. In any case they can do much damage, not only to other animals in play, but to the owner's clothes, particularly stockings.

They are best removed on the third or fourth day. It is probably better for a novice to get a knowledgeable friend or a veterinary surgeon to remove dew claws from a first litter. The operation should be watched carefully for future reference. It is easily and quickly done if someone is there to hold the puppies. The breeder with a little experience will soon find the technique of doing it single handed.

A pair of blunt-pointed, preferably short-bladed scissors

are needed, with a few pledgets of lint or cotton wool and a styptic to stop bleeding. Tincture of perchloride of iron is quite satisfactory.

The puppy should be held facing the operator, with the forelegs held out towards him. He must hold the leg gently but firmly with the left hand, spreading the dew claw slightly away from the leg, while with the right hand he places the open blades of the scissors flush with the leg, with the dew claw between the blades, as close as possible to the leg and parallel with it. A single closing of the scissor blades removes the entire digit at the joint. It is essential to remove it in this way, for if a small piece of the bone is left it will grow and be unsightly as well as troublesome.

Many puppies hardly notice this small operation, some may give a single cry, but it appears almost painless at this age. Any bleeding should be stopped by pressure with a pad of lint moistened with the preparation mentioned. The second dew claw should be removed and the pup returned to its bed while the next is taken up and dealt with. The bitch of course should have been taken well out of earshot before beginning the task.

When all have been done the pups should be checked over to be sure that no dew claw has been left, and that all bleeding has stopped. The bitch can then be allowed to return to her family and will notice nothing amiss.

The tiny wounds heal very quickly.

Eyes. Puppies' eyes begin to open about the tenth day, and by the end of the second week all should be open. During the process, and for a few days afterwards, the eye should not be exposed to strong light.

By this time shadowy spots will be appearing on the white coats with which the pups are born. Pigment will be spreading in nose and eye-rims in puppies which are not born with these parts fully pigmented.

Nails. From about a week after birth, to the age at which the puppies run about, preferably on a hard surface, nails should be systematically trimmed. They grow very quickly into hooked, sharply pointed weapons which can inflict considerable damage, not only on the bitch, but on their litter-mates during the period in which they drag themselves about and claw their way to the bitch over the backs of other puppies. Considerable sores can be produced in this way, which are always stated, even by veterinary surgeons, to be eczema.

If the sharp points are removed from the nails the sores will disappear, and even if nothing is done they heal as soon as the puppies are on their legs. But the dam can become very badly scratched by untrimmed claws, and if any bitch becomes disagreeable and refuses to feed her puppies it is wise to examine her to see whether she is wounded, and in any case to trim the puppies' nails. An ordinary pair of nail scissors is needed, and care should be taken not to cut into the pink part of the nail. If the nail is black, the curved tip can still be removed safely. Nails grow so quickly that trimming must be done at least every week, sometimes more often. When the pups are running about, and especially on a hard surface, nails wear themselves down naturally.

Every puppy house should have an enclosed run attached to it and I have always found concrete to be perfectly satisfactory. It is easily kept clean, it brings puppies up on their feet and wears down their nails well, and has fewer if any drawbacks compared with other forms of surface. Gravel is dirty and all puppies tend to swallow stones; turf is dirty in wet weather and very bad for feet.

When pups are brought up in the house, arrangements are more difficult and as good a run as possible must be arranged.

While the puppies remain in their box the bitch looks after the cleanliness, clearing up anything that is passed. As soon as they are running about, the first stage of house training can begin. Most puppies are reluctant to soil their beds after the first three weeks, and advantage can be taken of this by having a heap of sawdust in one corner of their quarters, and lifting the pup on to it immediately after every meal. The natural rhythm of evacuations in young puppies is for the bowel to act after every feed, the entry of food into the stomach setting off this chain of events. Later in life the process becomes less frequent, but often at about the same time daily, which can be very useful in a house dog.

Rearing a little is a delightful experience, and many

Dalmatian breeders spend a lot of time with their puppies, an education for them as well as for the youngsters.

Ideally, a time should be set aside every day when each puppy, from the age of three weeks, is picked up and cuddled and caressed and talked to quietly, so that they learn to enjoy close human contact and handling. Rearing a litter well is a very expensive and time-consuming business and should only be undertaken by someone who can give it the necessary devotion.

Worming. It is rare for any litter to reach the age of seven weeks without any signs of the roundworms which infest puppies, in spite of what the apostles of so-called natural rearing may say or do in the matter of treatment. A well-managed litter, however, will not often need dosing before that age, though this must be done if large numbers of worms are present. They can be identified by their appearance, which is not unlike that of an earthworm, but rather more slender and pointed. The roundworm always coils itself into a spiral. A badly infested puppy becomes unthrifty, with a staring coat, diarrhoea, and the passage of worms in masses.

An early sign of worm infestation is a tendency to develop a pot belly after every feed; the present of slimy mucus in the motions is usually the first sign with slowing up of progress. A standstill in weight will follow unless the worms are removed.

Expert advice should always be sought from the veterinary surgeon when puppies need worming. The best and most effective remedies cannot be bought over the counter at a chemist's, they must be obtained from the professional man and instructions must be faithfully observed.

Modern remedies are a great advance on the more old fashioned, and one of the gains is that previous fasting is rarely needed.

The medicine is usually given in capsule form. The puppy should be held on a table, the capsule moistened in water and slipped to the very back of the tongue; if it is placed farther forward the puppy has no difficulty in ejecting it immediately. Placed far back with the mouth immediately closed and held shut, the pup will have to swallow the dose, and the act of swallowing is easily recognized. Puppies can be very clever at holding the dose in the mouth until put down and then getting rid of it, and it is then of course impossible to know which puppy has not had its dose.

It is wise to stay with the litter for an hour or two in case of vomiting which may occur and which leads to the same problem.

Plenty of warning is usually given before a puppy vomits; it should be picked up at once and the mouth held firmly shut. Any regurgitated matter will then have to be swallowed again.

Worms may be passed for about twenty-four hours. With a heavy infestation it is wise to repeat the dose in a fortnight's time. No puppy should be sold before it has been wormed.

Buyers of eight-week-old puppies should be told of the great importance of vaccination against the virus diseases of distemper/hardpad, canine virus hepatitis, leptospiral jaundice and parvovirus. The advent of the latter early in the present decade, when many thousands of dogs died, necessitated a complete re-think on inoculations, as those already in use were not effective. Early problems have now been ironed out and new combinations of vaccine evolved which give excellent cover against all the infections mentioned above. Many veterinery surgeons now prefer to delay the first inoculation beyond eight weeks to enable the puppy to outgrow the maternal immunity. This means that extra care is needed to prevent the puppy bought at eight weeks coming in contact with possible sources of infection.

It should be emphasized again that the future physical condition, health, and temperament of puppies depends to a great extent on the feeding and general management during the early weeks of life.

However good its inheritance may be in both these respects, hereditary potentialities can be fulfilled only if environment, in the widest sense of the word, is favourable. A good environment in the case of puppies is one in which the dam is a sensible and devoted mother; the feeding throughout is such as to provide all the ingredients of a correct diet, giving adequate nourishment for the growing body with all its needs; freedom and room for play, and the exercise this involves, are ensured; and relations between the puppies and humans are those of affection and understanding.

SOME INCIDENTALS OF BREEDING

Deafness. This has been already mentioned. Our concern here is to find means of identifying a deaf puppy in the litter. The hereditary character of the defect is considered in Chapter 12.

It is not difficult to suspect that a puppy is deaf if the possibility is borne in mind, and fortunately deafness can be established before the puppy is old enough to be sold.

Suspicion must be aroused if one or, perhaps, two puppies are always the last to get out of the nest for food. Deaf puppies take no notice of doors opening or closing or any of the normal sounds, food bowls rattling, talking, or whistling. The deaf pup is unresponsive to the sounds to which normally hearing puppies react immediately by lifting their heads and moving.

A deaf puppy lying in a heap with others will of course be roused by their movements, but lying alone it will take no notice of any sounds at all. Once such a puppy has been noticed, and it has been established that the unresponsive puppy is always the same one, tests of various kinds can be made by the breeder, and it is often possible for him to be quite certain that the puppy is deaf. Should there be any doubt at all veterinary help should be sought, and if the diagnosis is confirmed there is only one thing to do, hard as it is, for no deaf puppy should be sold or given away, for its own sake, as well as that of the breed.

Tests which may be used are various noises; the rattle of a spoon on a food bowl; whistles of varying notes, the Acme silent whistle is excellent; doors opening and shutting noisily; a voice calling, and so on. The noises must be varied as much as possible and the same noise should never be used for long at a time. Even a puppy with normal hearing will quickly become used to the same stimulus and cease to respond. It is in fact a law of nature, which functions on both the physical and psychological plane, that any stimulus loses its effect if too often repeated.

A puppy which consistently fails to respond to any variety of aural stimulus after several days' observation and testing must be considered deaf, and a veterinary surgeon should be asked to put it down.

In addition to the above mentioned totally deaf puppy, for which the course of action is clear, there is the occasional puppy with a partial hearing loss. In some cases only one ear is affected. This makes detection much more difficult as the pup gives signs of hearing sounds on some occasions but not on others. One long-experienced breeder had a saying 'where there is doubt, there is deafness', a very sound rule-of-thumb diagnosis. It is unwise to let sentiment overrule prudence in these cases as puppies unable to hear properly cannot give the alert responsive companionship so important to their owners.

A deaf Dalmatian is a pathetic object, it is exceedingly difficult to train for once out of sight of the owner no sort of control is possible. Should it fall into the hands of anyone ignorant of its defect it will be considered stupid and 'naughty', and probably punished, sometimes roughly treated. There is only one solution for these handicapped puppies, and at this age it is essential for a veterinary surgeon to destroy them. Should a deaf puppy be inadvertently sold, the breeder should take it back and have it put down, replacing it with another normally hearing puppy, or refunding the price paid. It is a bad mark for any breeder who sells one, for he is supposed to know his business.

Hand Rearing. Dalmatians have very large litters. One of twelve puppies and upwards is common, and to allow one bitch to try to rear so many is asking for trouble for both dam and litter.

The more commercially minded breeders are sometimes tempted to this course. They should remember that even from the financial angle puppies from the time they are weaned cost a great deal of money to feed properly in such numbers. A badly reared Dalmatian is a sorry sight and no credit to its breeder or to the breed. Reputations whether as good breeders or as indifferent breeders are soon acquired, and the breeder's reputation, whether he breeds as a hobby or for other reasons, is his most important asset.

The experienced breeder will keep only as many puppies as his bitch can rear comfortably, without loss of condition to herself or detriment to the puppies' health and nutrition and no bitch should be mated at consecutive seasons unless for exceptional reasons.

Should the bitch be unable to feed her puppies, or should it be essential for some reason to keep more than seven or eight, some help must be given. Another bitch will often have supplies of milk at the time she would have whelped had she been mated. If she will accept two or three puppies the dam's burden will be lightened. The approach with a second bitch must be cautious. If she licks any puppies offered to her, they will probably be accepted, especially if she has had litters of her own and has proved a good mother, as indeed most Dalmatian bitches are.

In the sad case of orphaned puppies hand feeding will be inevitable unless a foster-mother can be secured, and the right foster-mother is not always easy to find.

If hand feeding is needed, it must be recognized as an arduous task. Two-hourly feeds day and night are necessary for the first week. The reinforced milk already described is quite suitable for this. The old-fashioned fountain-pen filler can be used if such a thing is still to be found, or some other form of dropping apparatus can be used. After a week a premature babies' feeding bottle is useful but the teat of this is too large for newly born puppies.

Warmth is the first essential. A covered box or basket can be used, well lined and draughtproof. Some form of heating is needed, and an infra-red lamp suspended over the bed is excellent; it must be used at the height recommended.

The bitch herself cares for normally fed puppies by licking to stimulate urination and defecation. This stimulation must be carried out by the breeder, with a light massage over the abdomen by a finger wrapped in some damp material.

The puppies must be kept clean, and the bedding changed as often as necessary, at least once daily.

After the first week feeds can be reduced to three-hourly intervals and puppies can be taught to lap for themselves as early as possible. Since the puppies will not be receiving the normal supplies of Vitamin A and D from their dam, one drop of halibut-liver oil should be given daily, and preferably dropped onto the mouth of each puppy.

An alternative to this method is a foster-mother, and she should have whelped at about the same time as the puppies' dam.

The average Dalmatian breeder would be wise to keep only the number of puppies his bitch can rear easily without extraneous help.

The Broody Bitch. This is the name often given to those bitches, and they are many, which behave as if they were going to have puppies at the time these would have been born had the bitches been mated. The description is apt, for their behaviour is much like that of a broody hen. These bitches make a nest and retire to it, with whatever handy object they can find to mother – fur gloves are very popular, and are never destroyed during this period, but cherished jealously. A sign that the condition is wearing off in Dalmatians is the loss of interest in these objects. A little milk may be produced, and it is these bitches which often take over puppies, whereupon the milk supply becomes more plentiful and the puppies are reared as if the bitch were their dam.

The condition is due to stimulation by some of the normal reproductive hormones. It usually lasts for about two weeks or so, then the bitch gradually returns to normal, unless she has been given puppies to rear.

There is usually no difficulty with the milk, but if it is excessive and the breasts swollen and hard, a little must be drawn off to relieve tension. This should be avoided if possible as it increases milk secretion. No rubbing or massage should be allowed for the same reason.

Broodiness is not the condition in which a mated bitch appears in every way to be pregnant for most of the normal gestation period. The bitch may in fact be pregnant. However, as the time of whelping draws near, the signs become less, no movements of puppies are to be seen, and no whelping takes place.

In such cases the embryonic puppies usually die and are absorbed by the tissues of the bitch. This constitutes a false pregnancy.

The cause may be an illness during pregnancy, with a toxic condition which affects the unborn puppies and kills them; their death may also be due to lack of vitality necessary for survival through some hereditary weakness.

Such genetic conditions are known in other species, they are due to what are called 'lethal' genes, that is genes (usually recessive) the presence of which in duplicate is incompatible with life. Such lethal genes are known in the mouse. A gene for the colour yellow, inherited from both parents, inevitably causes the death of the embryo mice, with the result that no yellow mice are ever seen though yellow exists as a coat colour in the species.

10

The Dalmatian Abroad

This chapter is intended to include Dalmatian clubs all over the world, and any countries which have organized Dalmatian activities. There may be others of which I know nothing and if so I apologize for this.

There is a bond of union between Dalmatian clubs wherever they may be, apart from the love of Dalmatians which unites them. This is the possession of what is very nearly a common standard, based on the English standard of 1890, from which all others are derived, and on its modern version, the Kennel Club standard of 1950. The American standard has made a few radical alterations recently, and the true international standard which looked so near achievement has now eluded us, but in spite of this all standards have a common basis and in essence the American is not far from the rest.

Dalmatian organizations will be considered in a rough order of seniority which may not be accurate to a year or so.

AMERICA

The Dalmatian Club of America was mooted in 1904 and formed officially in 1905. This is the parent Dalmatian Club of the United States, with a number of regional clubs which were formed later under its wing. Thanks to the late Mr H. Fred Lauer, a well-known enthusiast of the period, who in 1907 wrote a small booklet entitled *Dalmatians*, we know something about the early history of the breed in America. Another booklet published recently by the Dalmatian Club of America contains an excellent article on early history of the club, of which Mrs Bonney, a very old friend of all English Dalmatian enthusiasts, is one of the most senior members.

Its first President was Alfred Maclay, Harry T. Peters was Vice-President, and J. Sergeant Price Jr. was Secretary-Treasurer. The club adopted the English standard of 1890 with some variations. Mr Lauer wrote about it as follows:

'The following is a description and standard recommended by the American Dalmatian Club and is that of the English Dalmatian Club, but is not to the liking of a great many members of the Club, and we hope in the future it will have various changes, for it is not at all suitable for letting a novice know what is wanted or needed in true-type Dalmatians.'

There are a number of illustrations in this book which are of great interest. Some dogs are mentioned as being imported, though no breeder or country is mentioned. However, some prefixes are English, notably the Rugby prefix of the late Mrs Bedwell, whose dogs were of high quality for the period. Dogs in America as in England have greatly improved in many ways since that day. Lauer quotes briefly some of the supposed origins of the breed, though he gives no authority for his information. He mentions the legend of absence of scenting power in Dalmatians and evidently agrees with it, for he writes:

'While it is not improbable that the breed was originally used for sporting purposes, and indeed their appearance seems to indicate that generations ago they sprang from some of the branches of the Pointer family, still so long a time has elapsed since these conditions that they seem to have lost their noses.'

This author also accepts without question that Dalmatians came originally from Dalmatia and writes:

'Their unique appearance and great ability to run made them very popular with travellers from England and the Continent, who passed through Dalmatia, and those in need of a companion or a dog to guard them on their journey, saw quickly that this dog was particularly adapted to their needs.'

On the face of it this story seems highly improbable, and we may perhaps suppose that Lauer thought it would lend a little life to the bare bones of Dalmatian history. However, though little or no evidence is to be found for this theory of the origin of the breed, the name itself lends a certain validity to the view that it had something to do with Dalmatia. The difficulty is that throughout the centuries the breed had been known in Europe and England, as evidence from paintings of the past shows, but in no case was the name of Dalmatian applied to it before the *History of Quadrupeds* by Bewick and Beilby in the last decade of the eighteenth century. The third edition of this book was published in 1791.

Lauer wrote that the Dalmatian had been known in America for centuries, though again he does not give his authority for this statement, but that they were rare until about five years before the time at which he wrote (1907). He quotes our English authors though he does not mention their nationality, and it seems probable from his text that he did not himself read the originals, for they are not always accurately reported.

However this may be, Lauer was a well-known breeder of his day with a great love of the breed and his book must have done a great deal for Dalmatians and the Dalmatian Club of America in its early days, besides being an invaluable historical record of its period.

From the foundation twenty-six members in 1905 the number rose steadily to a peak of 8623 in 1972. This levelled off over the next few years, a tendency applauded by all who care for the good of the breed. There are now twenty-four Dalmatian Clubs in the USA in addition to the DCA which is regarded as the national breed club by the AKC. In its hands rests control of the standard and welfare of the breed. Its President is Mr Alfred E. Treen.

In 1950 the Dalmatian Club of America published a revised edition of its standard which in most respects resembled the original, though a clause on gait was included, which is certainly needed in a road-going dog. Strangely enough no English standard has mentioned this

important point and any future revision should include
it.

The American clause on gait reads:

'Length of stride should be in proportion to the size of the
dog, steady in rhythm of 1, 2, 3, 4 as in cadence count in
military drill. Front legs should not paddle, nor should there
be a straddling appearance. Hind legs should neither cross
nor weave. Judges should be able to see each leg move with
no interference from another leg; drive and reach are
most desirable.'

There is much to agree with in this clause, though
'cadence drill' is not familiar to English readers and in fact
when a dog moves away from the judge in a straight line, the
hind legs conceal the fore, if they are directly behind the latter
as we think they should be.

While discussing this topic we must mention the latest
revision of the American standard which received the
approval of the American Kennel Club early in 1963. As this
standard is of great importance to breeders here in England,
who export dogs to the States, it is given in full.

Description and Standard of the Dalmatian
as adopted by the Dalmatian Club of America
at the Annual Meeting held 12 February 1962

The Dalmatian should represent a strong muscular and active dog;
poised and alert; free of shyness; intelligent in expression; symmetrical
in outline and free from coarseness and lumber. He should be capable
of great endurance, combined with a fair amount of speed.

The Head should be of fair length, the skull flat, proportionately
broad between the ears, and moderately well defined at the temples,
and not in one straight line from the nose to the occiput bone as
required in a Bull Terrier. It should be entirely free from wrinkle.

The Muzzle should be long and powerful – the lips clean. The mouth
should have a scissors bite. Never undershot or overshot. It is permiss-
ible to trim whiskers.

Eyes should be set moderately well apart, and of medium size, round
bright, and sparkling, with an intelligent expression; their color
greatly depending on the markings of the dog. In the black-spotted
variety the eyes should be dark (black or brown or blue). In the liver-

spotted variety they should be lighter than in the black-spotted variety (golden or light brown or blue).

The rim round the eyes in the black-spotted variety should be black; in the liver-spotted variety, brown. Never flesh-colored in either. Lack of pigment a major fault.

The Ears should be set on rather high, of moderate size, rather wide at the base and gradually tapering to a rounded point. They should be carried close to the head, be thin and fine in texture, and preferably spotted.

The Nose in the black-spotted variety should always be black; in the liver-spotted variety always brown. A butterfly or flesh-colored nose is a major fault.

Neck and Shoulders. The neck should be fairly long, nicely arched, light and tapering, and entirely free from throatiness. The shoulders should be oblique, clean, and muscular, denoting speed.

Body, Back, Chest, and Loins. The chest should not be too wide, but very deep and capacious, ribs well sprung, but never rounded like barrel hoops (which would indicate want of speed). Back powerful, loins strong, muscular, and slightly arched.

Legs and Feet of great importance. The forelegs should be straight, strong, and heavy in bone; elbows close to body; feet compact, well-arched toes and tough elastic pads. In the hind legs the muscles should be clean, though well defined; the hocks well let down. Dew claws may be removed from the legs.

Nails. In the black-spotted variety black and white, or a nail may be both black and white. In the liver-spotted variety brown or white, or a nail may be both brown and white.

Gait. Length of stride should be in proportion to the size of the dog; steady in rhythm of 1, 2, 3, 4 as in the cadence count in military drill. Front legs should not paddle, nor should there be a straddling appearance. Hind legs should neither cross nor weave; judges should be able to see each leg move with no interference of another leg. Drive and reach are most desirable. Cow hocks are a major fault.

The Tail should ideally reach the hock joint, strong at the insertion, and tapering towards the end, free from coarseness. It should not be inserted too low down, but carried with a slight curve upward, and never curled.

The Coat should be short, hard, dense, and fine, sleek and glossy in appearance, but neither woolly nor silky.

Color and Markings are most important points. The ground color in both varieties should be pure white, very decided, and not intermixed. The color of the spots in the black-spotted variety should be dense black; in the liver-spotted variety they should be liver brown. The spots should not intermingle, but be as round and well defined as possible, the more distinct the better. In size they should be from that of a dime to a half-dollar. The spots on the face, head, ears, legs, and tail to be smaller than those on the body.

Patches and any other color markings other than black or liver constitute a disqualification. A true patch is a solid sharply defined mass of black or liver that is appreciably larger than any of the markings on the dog. Several spots that are so adjacent that they actually touch one another at their edges do not constitute a patch.

Size. The desirable height of dogs and bitches is between 19 and 23 inches at the withers, and any dog over 24 inches at the withers is to be disqualified.

Disqualifications
> Any color other than black or liver.
> Any size over twenty-four inches at the withers.
> Patches.
> Tri-colors.
> Undershot or Overshot bites.

Major Faults
> Butterfly or flesh-colored nose.
> Cow Hocks.
> Flat Feet.
> Lack of pigment in eye-rims.
> Shyness.
> Trichiasis (abnormal position or direction of the eyelashes).

Faults
> Ring or low-set tail.
> Undersize or oversize.

Scale of Points

	Value
Body, Back, Chest, and Loins	10
Coat	5
Color and Markings	25
Ears	5
Gait	10
Head and Eyes	10
Legs and Feet	10
Neck and Shoulders	10
Size and Symmetry, etc.	10
Tail	5
Grand Total	100

There are some additions to this standard which would be welcomed by British breeders. The first is the sentence on shyness, the second is a clause on gait, the third is a definition of a patch. I am not sure, however, that the American definition is entirely reliable for one does occasionally see an area of colour considerably larger than other markings on the dog, and the line between this and a patch is debatable. I remember one well-known winning bitch in the mmediate post-war period, bred and shown by an experienced breeder, with just such a marking on one flank, and it was never suggested that this was a patch.

One could have wished that the intolerable wordiness of our standard in some clauses could have been avoided in any new version, and the description of coat texture have been more realistic.

One other point might be mentioned. The numerical standard value of points allows ten out of every hundred for 'size, symmetry, etc.' But a disqualification on size will mean that a dog over 90 per cent perfect will be automatically disqualified. This I find difficult to understand.

Members of the Dalmatian Club of America support all general championship shows in the States and have a fine record. Several, among whom the most prominent is Mrs L. Allman*, are well known as consistent Group winners, and this award I understand carries far more prestige than best of breed wins.

To campaign a Dalmatian in the United States involves an immense amount of travelling all over that vast country.

Showing is largely entrusted to professional handlers as in the case of most terrier breeds here.

The Dalmatian Club of America holds an annual specialty show which is very popular. Classes in the States are fewer and less complicated than our own; they include a class for 'champions only', something that is often advocated here.

In view of the smaller number of classes, entries are naturally lower than those in this country.

One of the most active regional Dalmatian clubs in the

* Now Mrs Ratner.

United States is the Dalmatian Club of Southern California founded in 1949. Fifteen members and prospective members attended the first meeting. The first President was Mr Alvin J. Moneybrake Jr., the first Vice-President was Mr Leyland Berriman, and the first Secretary-Treasurer was Mrs Jeffrey Sidebotham. The new club's first specialty show was held in September 1950. This club clearly attracted enthusiastic and active members and so it has continued to the present day. The Dalmatian Club of Southern California holds an annual breed show in conjunction with an all-breed show, as well as an annual Puppy Match. It also issues a most interesting Newsletter entitled *The Splatter*. The club secretary is Janet Smith.

The Chicagoland Dalmatian Club is another keen and active club which is very go-ahead under Mrs Barbara Peters. She is not only an excellent president but a very good breeder. In a country as large as the United States the need for regional clubs is obvious. Others are those of North California and Southern New England.

In a country the size of America such regional clubs must be essential. Others include those of Northern California and of Southern New England.

Mention must be made of the various activities of American Dalmatians. They used to accompany fire engines when they went to fires; they are trained in coaching and trials are held in this traditional Dalmatian occupation; they are far more numerous in Obedience training and tests than are our English Dalmatians, something to be regretted in this country for Dalmatians are among the most attractive breeds working in this branch and always a pleasure to watch because of their gaiety and obvious enjoyment in working.

For years past many Dalmatians have been exported from this country to America and most have been successful there both in the show-ring and as breeding stock.

English breeders must keep up a high standard in exported stock, brearing always in mind the provisions of the new American Dalmatian standard.

GERMANY

To judge by the Dalmatians included in pictures in Continental galleries, especially in Germany, in the main by Dutch painters, they must have been known in Europe for several hundred years. They were probably one of the many hound breeds of the period, for they are most often shown in sporting paintings.

The German Dalmatian Club is the next in order of seniority. It was founded in 1920. Its object, as that of all other Dalmatian clubs, is to foster the interest of the breed. In addition it acknowledges the authority of the Fédération Cynologique Internationale, and agrees to protect the purity of the breed and to judge it according to the standards laid down by this body. The FCI, as it is always called, is the ruling authority of canine affairs on the Continent, to which National Canine Authorities are subordinated in certain matters, such as standards. The national German authority, The Union of German Canine Organizations (Der Verband für das Deutsche Hundewesen), corresponds to some extent to our own Kennel Club, though without its ultimate authority in all matters. This belongs to the FCI Stud Books and registrations, however, are the province of the breed clubs themselves. All litters must be notified to the club official responsible for registration; all live puppies must be registered, and by their breeder. Breeding itself is fairly strictly controlled. From a first litter in Germany only four puppies may be retained, and only six from subsequent litters.

The FCI has the ultimate control over standards, which it issues to all European countries which recognize its sovereignty and, as far as I know, this includes all with any organized canine activities. Our own Kennel Club does not recognize the authority of the FCI though it maintains friendly relations with it.

The original German standard for Dalmatians, issued by the FCI, was a translation of the English standard, though the arrangement of the clauses was different from ours. A standard height was included: 58–60 cm for dogs, 50–54 cm for bitches; roughly speaking this amounts to about 19½–24 inches minimum and maximum.

However, in 1955 the FCI decided to re-issue all standards according to their countries of origin, and the country of Dalmatian origin was stated to be Jugoslavia. How this was decided is difficult to understand unless the name Dalmatian was the sole criterion. Our own standard and that of the Basenji were the only two not issued in the language of their country of origin, for obvious reasons, they were issued in French. It is improbable that any Dalmatian standard exists in Jugoslavia, for as far as I am aware, and several Dalmatian lovers have investigated this, there is no Dalmatian organization and no longer any Dalmatians.*

This standard put the clock back many years as far as the progress of the breed is concerned. It still included translations of considerable parts of the English standard but permitted patches on both sides of the head and equally one completely black or brown cheek. A completely brown or black head and large black or brown patches elsewhere on the body were to be faults. Eye-rims could be unpigmented in Dalmatians with 'plain' (unspotted) faces.

There was much dismay in European countries with Dalmatian clubs as can well be imagined, and I was approached to see whether the Kennel Club could not protest. However, naturally this was impossible since it is not a member of the FCI. Continental countries therefore tacitly ignored this absurd standard, and continued to judge according to the older and more sensible one used before.

Eventually, in February 1961, the 1955 Dalmatian standard was withdrawn by the FCI and a new one substituted. This was a literal translation of the 1950 English standard (though some clauses were rearranged), with two differences. The first was the addition of the word 'the', to the clause stating that colour and markings are most important points, reading 'colour and markings are the most important points', the second was a standard of height as before.

Although this standard is still described as that of

---

* There are now a number of Dalmatians in Jugoslavia.

Jugoslavia, I have found it rather amusing that the size of the spots is given as 'sixpence and a florin' translated into centimetres in a footnote.

As most people know, the absence of even one pre-molar tooth is regarded in Germany as a most serious fault and a sign of degeneration, though not everyone agrees with this view. It is curious therefore that no mention of teeth was made in the three FCI standards, and though they are included in the current standard of 1961, the description is a literal translation of the clause on teeth in the English standard of 1950.

The German Dalmatian Club has approximately 1186 members, including many in other countries. Some are also members of the British Dalmatian Club. The President is Mr E. Schuster and the Secretary Dipl.Ing. A. Ronneberg.

Dalmatians in Germany have improved in all respects on those I judged at Frankfurt in 1960. Conformation and decoration were both good and temperament in particular had much improved.

Dalmatian owners in Germany are more interested in Obedience than our own. Unlike ours, their dogs are not discouraged from aggressiveness. Even in the show-ring, the judge has to keep a close eye on the dog he is examining, and a sign 'Biter' above a bench is quite common. Not all Dalmatians show this aggressiveness, but it does not seem to be frowned on.

Germans are serious breeders and take great trouble over choosing the right partners in their matings. Their regulations seem to me to tend to concentrate on the absence of faults rather than on the presence of virtues but that is their point of view. I believe my view that absence of certain faults does not of necessity result in a good Dalmatian is shared by by most English breeders of experience.

LUXEMBOURG

The Luxembourg Dalmatian Club was formed in 1973 by a small band of enthusiasts. Today it can boast almost a hundred home members and an equal number of foreign associate members. The club organizes a number of events and produces an excellent newsletter. The President is Mme Barbara Kacens.

HUNGARY

The Hungarian Club has a growing and enthusiastic membership giving support for their shows and activities. The Hon. Secretary is Gyula Ceskó Esq.

MEXICO

A strong Dalmatian Club exists in Mexico under the Presidency of Raymond F. Fitzsimmons, with more than sixty members giving support to shows and other club events.

AUSTRALIA

I am indebted to Mr Colin Nelson, formerly Honorary Secretary of the Dalmatian Club of Australia, for much of this section, and through him, to Mr and Mrs James Macdougal among the most senior and important people in the history of the breed in Australia. Mr R. Grenyer is now the Secretary.

Dalmatians were known in Australia prior to 1899, although they were rare and each dog created much interest on this account.

Mr James Macdougal's father had a Dalmatian in Brisbane in 1897, and in 1899 Mr H. Arrowsmith made canine history in Australia by entering five Dalmatians at Sydney Royal Show.

Mr Arrowsmith continued to keep the breed before the public until 1911, but from that year on there is no information until 1930, when Mr and Mrs Edward Hirst of Springmead Farm, Ingleburn, New South Wales, two more names famous in the breed, began a new Dalmatian era by importing Quintus of Caefel and Florenza. The Caefel prefix was well known in England in the early thirties, it was that of Captain (now Sir Ambrose) Keevil. Soon after this Mr A. J. O'Driscoll imported two Goworths from the late Mrs Wigglesworth, Goworth Eclipse and Goworth Maria.

In 1934 Mrs James Macdougal took back two from England to found her famous Korchula Kennel, Dauntless Dal from the Coelan Kennel of Miss Millie Stephens, and Adriatic Queen, but the latter was not a success in any capacity. Dauntless Dal proved of great value to the breed.

English exports to Australia have continued to the present time and many famous English kennels are represented. The post-war Dalmatians which were sent to Australia include Postchaise Clarissa, from Mr Eddie Davies to Mr Frank Johnson of New South Wales, Chorister of Fenmere from Miss Whitton and Kerford Kyle, from the late Mrs Stratford, both to Mrs Mackinolty of New South Wales, and most recent of all, Colonsay Roll of the Dice from Miss Macfie to Mr C. Nelson. This bitch is now an Australian champion and has produced excellent litters.

The best English blood is represented in the many Dalmatians exported to Australia during the past thirty years.

In 1942 it was felt that a specialist club was needed to further the interests of Dalmatians in Australia and at a meeting in January 1943, twenty-five enthusiastic supporters of the breed founded the Dalmatian Club of Australia. The new club flourished, entries at shows were excellent, and their club exercised a powerful influence on the Australian canine world, until, in 1948, when owing to indiscriminate breeding by several large commercial breeders, the balance of popularity tipped and entries at shows dropped to a very low figure and remained so with slight fluctuations until 1958.

Since that year Dalmatians have slowly climbed back and are gaining more and more popularity each successive year. Average entries at shows are now around the figure of fifty;

at one recent show in New South Wales the entry was seventy-three and the club membership in 1963 exceeded one hundred.

In other parts of Australia, however, Dalmatians have not flourished to quite the same extent, though in Victoria there is now a thriving club under the Presidency of Mr Neil Watkins. A championship show is enthusiastically supported as well as numerous educational and social events. The Club also produces a lively newsletter.

There is no doubt of the progress of Dalmatians in Australia, quality is being maintained at the expense of numbers and indiscriminate breeding is strongly discouraged by the club. Faults are becoming fewer, deafness is now almost unknown, pigmentation has greatly improved, and wall eyes are rare enough for exhibitors of three or four years' experience never to have seen them. Mr Nelson feels that, as in many overseas countries, oversize and undersize are still problems.

This short history of the Dalmatian Club of Australia's foundation and its success, including the publication of an excellent monthly newsletter entitled *News Spots* edited by Mr Nelson, the enthusiasm of its officers and its members, and their devotion to the best ideals of the breed, all these are a guarantee of the continued success of Dalmatians in Australia.

NEW ZEALAND

The Dalmatian Club of New Zealand can boast an enthusiastic membership under the Presidency of Mr Dennis Rowlands, with Mrs Karen Clayton as Secretary. Numerous shows and events are well suported and there is a strong emphasis on educational and welfare projects. An excellent bi-monthly newsletter, 'Spot on News', is appreciated by the somewhat wide-flung membership. The club suffered a grievous loss in the tragic death in 1985 of one of its leading members, Dr Margaret Topping, whose enthusiasm and knowledge of genetics had done much to encourage sound breeding, and the importing of dogs of top British bloodlines.

CANADA

The Dalmatian Club of Canada, President Mrs Monica Brooks and Secretary Mrs Penny Paul, caters for a very wide-flung area. It has representatives in all its regions and produces an excellent newsletter, 'Transcandals'.

HOLLAND

Dalmatians were not common in Holland before the 1939–45 War and during the period of occupation from 1940 to 1945 conditions were so difficult that few dogs of the rarer breeds survived.

When peace came, even though conditions were still far from normal, Dalmatian lovers in Holland looked about them to discover the state of the breed. They found that on the whole their best pre-war Dalmatians were no longer alive, and that very few animals were available to rebuild the breed.

This survey took time, but by 1947 it was clear that enough people in Holland were interested in Dalmatians to form a breed club and in that year, at a meeting in Utrecht in November, the Netherlands Dalmatian Club was born. Those present at this meeting included many of the experienced breeders of today. The ladies were: Mrs de Laitte, Mrs Oppelaar, Mrs Key, Mrs Hoogendijk-Vierdag, Miss Breukink (now Mrs van Lulofs Umbgrove), Mrs Heykoop, Mrs Carp, and Mrs Kloppenburg. The gentlemen were: Mr Duiker, Mr de Graaff, Mr van Unen, Mr van Middelkoop, Mr Mekil, and Mr Kloppenburg.

Mr Duiker was elected Chairman of the new club, Mr de Graaff Vice-Chairman, Mrs de Laitte Secretary, Mr van Unen Treasurer, and Mr van Middelkoop Director. Rules were formulated and the breed standard adopted was the English standard in its entirety.

Eventually it was decided that new blood must be obtained and Mrs de Laitte came to England. The result was that three dog puppies and one young bitch went to Holland during the next two years. The dogs were all of my Winnall strain and all closely related, the first a son of Winnall Joker, the other two sons of Ch. Winnall Elegance, Joker's daughter, one by his son, Ch. Ambala Sahib, the other by his grandson, Ch. Winnall Dazzler of Dalmally, Sahib's son. The bitch was Pengewood Blue Ribbon, a daughter of Ch. Norseman of Welfield and Opal of Welfield.

The death of Captain Verwey two years ago was a great loss to the Dutch breeders. His advice was invaluable.

An international continental champion must fulfil certain conditions. It must be best of sex, older than fifteen months, have won four international certificates in three different countries under three different judges. One CACIB must have been won in the country of origin; if not possible, in the country in which the owner lives. The qualification of 'Excellent' is essential.

The CACIB is short for 'Certificate d'Adaptation Cynologique Internationale de Beauté' or in English Certificate of Ability and Beauty.

Classes on the Continent are officially four in number, but a breeders' class is usually added for each sex, making six in all. These are Open, Youth (for animals under eighteen months of age), and Breeders.

In some countries, Germany for instance, the winner of a youth class may not be awarded the CACIB.

Classes are taken in the reverse order from our own, and as all dogs in the class have to be placed in their order of merit the judge's task is made easier by seeing the mature dogs first, for once given, the qualifications of excellent, very good, good, poor, are not reversed.

I had the honour of being asked to judge the first Dalmatian show in Holland in 1948. Every Dutch Dalmatian was present. Only a judge who saw those first exhibits can appreciate the advances made since those early days. There were many faults in those survivors of the war; faults of conformation, of decoration, and also of handling and presentation. In general it must be admitted that Continental exhibitors do not take handling or presentation very seriously and it is difficult to convince them that lack of these is a serious handicap to any dog, however good.

Even the best Dalmatian, if ungroomed, unwashed, and untrained, makes a poor impression, and a dog which cannot be handled and which is never still for a moment is difficult to assess. The Dutch have now learned this lesson and their Dalmatians have not only improved greatly but are also much better presented.

Shows themselves in Holland are extremely well managed and judges are treated with great consideration.

In 1950, when I judged the breed at the Winner show in Amsterdam, I found an improvement on 1948. When I again judged the Winner in 1960, the general improvement was surprising.

In the meantime the Netherlands Club had asked Miss Clay to judge the Winner of 1956, and Mrs Hamilton judged at The Hague in 1961.

Dutch breeders are entirely serious in their wish to improve their Dalmatians. Such single-mindedness, coupled with the excellent advice made available to them from Captain Verwey and their most experienced breeders, must produce good results, as indeed it does. I would say from what I have seen that the Dutch Dalmations are probably the best in Europe, and the best of them could compete here on equal terms.

During the period of the 1955 FCI Dalmatian standard, already mentioned, the Dutch judges and breeders held steadfastly to the standard they had adopted when the club was founded, and have been justified in the event.

It is impossible to mention the names of all the Dutch breeders whose activities have had such a good result. One more, however, must be named, Mrs van Gelderen-Parker. Although this lady no longer shows or breeds Dalmatians owing to the claims of a young family, she was one of the mainstays of the breed in Holland from the foundation of the Netherlands Club until recently; she has visited Cruft's with Mrs Oppelaar on a number of occasions and is known here to many friends.

Today, in 1987, the Nederlandse Club has 357 members and the President is Mrs H. W. Nellekoop-Transen and the Secretary is Mrs A. Morgans-Huisman.

FRANCE

Dalmatians have been known in France for centuries and there are some very good French breeders who breed very good dogs. Mme Garaix is the President of the Dalmatian Club of France and also undertakes much of the secretarial work of the Club in her home of the southern outskirts of Paris. She and her husband Dr Jean-Paul Garaix, are dedicated lovers of Dalmatians and have two house pets, both of which have been good winners. Their dog has sired several champions.

Five times yearly articles are written in *France Canine* by members on subjects of interest, with general information accompanied by photographs, and thus members keep in touch all the year round, for shows are not so frequent in France as they are here.

The Société Centrale Canine, corresponding to our Kennel Club, registers dogs, and in each year the initial letter of every dog registered has to be the same. Applications for registration have to be accompanied by nose prints, a method of identification as certain as that of fingerprints.

It is not easy to make a champion in France. The qualification for a champion is to have won three CACIB's (corresponding to our challenge certificates) at international shows organized by the Société Centrale Canine or a society affiliated to it, one of which must be won at the Paris Show.

As there is only one show in Paris each year this regulation means that only one new champion in each sex can be made each year. Should the certificate go to a foreign dog or bitch, or to one which is already a champion, then no new French champion will be made in that year.

It would seem that it is more difficult to become a champion in France than in any other country.

THE WEST INDIES

Dalmatians first appeared in Trinidad in the 1953–55 period, imported by Dr Cant. Later Sir Peter and Lady Watkin-Williams were posted to Trinidad and took with them Yarty Emperor of Elberton and Yarty Mona. Matings from these dogs with those owned by Dr Cant formed the foundation of all the local stock, with the welcome addition of Greenmount St Gregory, bred by Dr and Mrs Piper. Dalmatians increased in popularity over the next few years and in 1958 the Dalmatian Club of Trinidad and Tobago was formed with Mr Justice Blagden as its Chairman. Shows were held and challenge certificates awarded.

Unfortunately, with the unavoidable changes in the key figures due to postings to other areas, the fortunes of the club have fluctuated considerably.

AFRICA

There have been Dalmatians in many parts of Africa for years. The famous anthropologists Dr and Mrs Leakey had some with them in Kenya.

Rhodesia (now Zimbabwe) and South Africa were the areas of the most organized Dalmatian activity. This increased in the early post-war years when more English people settled in South Africa and Rhodesia and a number of good dogs were imported from Britain. A Dalmatian Club was formed on the initiative of Mrs Roseveare with Mrs Bell and Mrs Spencer and the English Standard was adopted. Many of its members also retained membership of the BDC.

SWITZERLAND

The Dalmatian Club of Switzerland, Schweiz-Dalmatiner Club, has 370 members and its President is Mr O. Rauch and Secretary Mrs E. Luisier.

SWEDEN

Founded in 1962 the Swedish Dalmatian Club boasts an approximate membership of 760 under the Chairmanship of Signe Fink with Ann-Katrin Johansson as Secretary.

This club owes much to one of its founder members, Mrs Hammarlund, whose knowledge and enthusiasm helped to establish it on a firm foundation. Her imports of good British and American dogs helped to raise the standard to the present high level. The club produces a first class newsletter and stages a number of well supported shows.

The Swedish Dalmatian Club has a large number of members. It produces a periodical newsletter which in size and contents surpasses most other of a like nature and must be of the greatest value to Swedish breeders, of whom Mrs Hammarlund and Miss Alkhagen are members of the British Dalmatian Club. Some excellent Dalmatians now exist in Sweden.

Many of our Continental friends come to this country to see English breeders and their dogs, and are old friends by now.

FINLAND

A Finnish club was formed in 1971 and has 380 enthusiastic supporters under its Chairman Pertti Kiho and Secretary Päivi Borgelin.

NORWAY

The Norsk Dalmatiner Klubb was founded in 1986 and now has a membership of approximately 250. Their Chairman is Helle Hoie and Secretary Anne Grete Nordlund.

A hallmark of these younger clubs is their enthusiasm and desire to improve their stock. Easier travel allows more of their members to visit shows in other countries including Britain and to see at first hand some of the world top Dalmatians.

INDONESIA

A Dalmatian club has been formed in Indonesia, by Dutch enthusiasts who took dogs with them from Holland. This club has a number of members of various races and there is

Ch. Spring Classic by Appaloosa (*Thomas Fall*)

Ch. Brythennek Basil Fawlty

Ch. Washakie Winona

Ch. Wardell Whatsizname

Ch. Tantivvey Target of Olbero

Ch. Illyricum Isa of Farforest (Photo taken at 8 years of age)
(*Anne Roslin-Williams*)

Ch. Horseman's Relay (*Diane Pearce*)

Int. Ch. Clydevale Mastermind (*Diane Pearce*)

much enthusiasm for a breed which tolerates a tropical climate so well.

With members so widely scattered over the world, the British Dalmatian Club can feel with some pride that it is practically an international institution.

11

The World Congress

The year 1980 was a momentous one in the annals of Dalmatians. In April of that year the first ever World Congress, under the title 'Dalmatians of the World Unite', was held at London's Kensington Close Hotel.

Sponsored by the British Dalmatian Club, the outstanding success of the Congress was in a large measure due to the initiative and enthusiasm of the then Secretary, Mrs Gwen Eady, and a specially appointed committee. Months of careful planning and preparation, not to mention untold hours of sheer hard work, came to fruition on Thursday 10 April when our President, Miss Betty Clay, welcomed several hundred delegates from worldwide Dalmatian Clubs.

Miss Clay then gave the first paper, on the subject of 'Dalmatians in Britain'. This was followed by an exposition from Mr Raymond Fitzsimmons of Mexico covering the subjects of Dalmatians in his country and others of the Latin American Continent and also the subject of the Breed Standard.

European and Continental Dalmatians were presented by Mrs Nancy van Gelderen-Parker of Holland with reference to their history and subsequent development in the various countries.

A fascinating paper on Dalmatians in New Zealand was given by Dr Margaret Topping (sadly, no longer with us) and we learned much of the spectacular improvement of the breed in that country as well as of the various problems which have arisen.

The very strong Dalmatian interest in Scandinavia was the subject of Mrs Ann-Marie Hammarlund's paper, covering as it did all the countries which make up this group. Mrs Hammarlund also dealt at length with the Swedish scientific studies of deafness in the breed.

Dalmatians in North America were the subject of a fascinating paper by Mrs Alfred Treen, giving the history of the breed in that vast continent up to its present flourishing condition, and also touching on problems which have arisen.

Mrs Mary Young gave an interesting history of the Dalmatian in Australia, its various ups and downs and its problems. The continent boasts five Dalmatian Clubs, all keen to promote and improve the state of the breed.

A most interesting and informative paper was given by Dr D. F. McDougall of the Animal Health Trust on the work being done in the field of kidney disease, and the results so far achieved.

The delegates dispersed with the hope expressed that a similar congress might be mounted every fourth year. In accordance with this, another successful congress was held in Philadelphia in 1984.

12
Dalmatian Inheritance

The science of heredity called Genetics is a new and rapidly growing branch of the biological sciences, that is to say those sciences which are concerned with living organisms. It is probably the most important of them all for it deals with life itself.

The name Genetics was coined because the unit of heredity was given the name of 'gene' (from the Greek Genos, a race). The gene is the hereditary factor which passes direct from parent to child and forms the sole connecting physical link between one generation and the next.*

There are thousands of genes in every individual and they transmit the entire inheritance. They are carried on bodies called Chromosomes, rather after the fashion of beads on a string. Both chromosomes and genes occur in pairs, one member of each pair being derived from the male parent, the other from the female. Inheritance therefore comes in equal amounts from both parents, even if not in actual effect as we shall see.

We are concerned here with a few simple principles of genetics to illustrate the hereditary conditions to be dealt with in this chapter.

We may ask whether genes from sire and dam are blended together to give an effect midway between that of the two halves of the gene pair. We may ask why related Dalmatians are on the whole more alike than those which are unrelated, and why, on the other hand, members of a litter are often so different in appearance seeing that their parentage is the same. We may ask how individual characters (the genetic

---

* Readers interested in the subject of genetics are referred to the Author's *Practical Dog Breeding and Genetics* (Popular Dogs).

name for characteristics) are passed on, and what exactly is meant by the term bloodlines, so often heard on the lips of dog breeders.

Every living organism which owes its existence to the union of individuals of two sexes receives half its inheritance from the male parent and half from the female, and so the sire and dam of every Dalmatian puppy each contributes half of its inheritance, passing on half only of their own to any individual puppy.

The minute sperm of the dog unites with the larger egg of the bitch at fertilization to produce the new individual.

The thoughtful reader will recognize a problem here. The union of two cells should give a double cell, twice the size of the two which formed it with twice the amount of cell contents including the chromosomes and genes.

The answer is that the sperm and the egg are in effect only half cells, they are called gametes and each possesses only half the normal number of chromosomes and genes. This process of cell division is complicated; it is called meiosis.

Before fertilization takes place the chromosomes and the genes they carry divide, one member of each pair goes to form one puppy, with a corresponding half from the second parent. The contribution from each parent is a sample half of its own inheritance, for chance determines which particular gene will pass into which puppy and which gene from the other partner will join it to become the second member of the gene pair.

Genes combine in many ways. In some gene pairs one member is able to suppress the effect of its partner. This was the first genetic discovery by Mendel, the father of genetics, long before the name gene was attached to what Mendel called a 'factor' of inheritance, which he postulated from the results of experiments on plants. His work was forgotten for over forty years, until it was discovered about the beginning of this century. In the meantime, English scientists had come to the same conclusions, though, owing to a knowledge of the cell and its behaviour by this time available but unknown in Mendel's day, they were able to go a stage further.

Mendel called his pair of factors, the one suppressing the

other, dominant and recessive. It follows that the recessive gene could give no signs of its presence when combined with a dominant partner. But, when this gene pair divides, the dominant member going to one puppy, the recessive to another, their effects will be different according to whether the new members are dominant or recessive. We shall see this illustrated when applying this principle practically.

The dominant-recessive relationship is the cause of many hereditary characters, notably faults, but it is far from being the only method by which genes work. Some can suppress the action of genes with which they are not paired, others can be suppressed. If suppressors they are termed epistatic, if suppressed, hypostatic.

Genes can modify the effect of other genes without having any other action, genes can dilute the effect of other genes, single pairs of genes can produce their effect, groups of genes may be needed to produce effects. In fact there are many ways in which genes can combine and many stages between the gene and the character for which it is responsible. The dominant-recessive relationship, so often thought of as being the most usual and the most important, is only one of many others.

A second great force has its share in influencing the effect of heredity. It is that of the external circumstances we call *Environment* which includes everything which influences life and development including events of the pre-natal period.

We can take growth as an example of the action of environment on heredity.

The hereditary pattern for this may be entirely favourable, but if the dog is starved of food of the right amount and quality, the hereditary pattern will be hampered and proper growth and development will not take place. On the other hand the best environment will not correct a bad hereditary pattern of growth.

We are now in a position to answer the questions put forward earlier. The term bloodlines has no exact meaning. It does not mean that inheritance, even of the closest relatives, need be entirely similar, except in the case of identical twins which are the product of a single fertilized egg.

As we have seen, genes are distributed among the progeny at random and it would be possible for two litter mates to differ very considerably in their inheritance. Related dogs are more alike on the whole; in spite of this random distribution of genes among progeny, they are more likely to possess genes in common because of the relationship. On the other hand litter-mates may show dissimilar characters because the sample each received from both parents may be quite different, on account of the separation of gene pairs at every mating and their recombination in the next generation.

Kalmus, in *Genetics* (Pelican 1948), has happily described this process as 'the shuffling and dealing' of genes in every generation.

Genes do not blend in the process of reproduction. Each maintains its own identity and is passed on unchanged with every generation. The sole exception is that of a mutation. This is a sudden, usually permanent, change in a gene which alters its effect so that the organism is different from the normal. Mutations are rare; they can be produced by radiation of various kinds.

How the single gene behaves in the next generation may depend on the second gene of the pair, inherited from the second parent.

Turning now to inheritance as it affects particular characters in Dalmatians, I start with something which is often the last point to be considered in a show dog, if it is indeed considered at all, and this is *Temperament*.

A fundamentally nervous temperament must be regarded as hereditary. It is true that nervousness in Dalmatians as in other breeds may be brought about by bad management and rough handling. Dalmatians are, I believe, especially susceptible to harsh treatment. They have not the 'toughness' of many terrier breeds for instance. They are slow to forget anything that has frightened or hurt them.

But the hereditarily nervous Dalmatian is frightened from the beginning and remains so, however well it is treated.

Fortunately these Dalmatians are rare, but they are a pitiful sight. Even small puppies will display fear with no apparent reason, and will refuse to respond to friendly advances.

Such a dog will, in later life, be terrified of the normal experiences which the Dalmatian with the typical happy disposition takes in its stride. Fresh faces, unusual noises, in fact many circumstances of normal life terrify the unfortunate animal. One can only be sorry for them in their real suffering. Life must be one long nightmare of fear for these unhappy dogs. Pathological fear, distrust, and nervousness are strongly hereditary.

Such temperaments are as great a handicap to the pet dog as they are to those which are shown and every attempt should be made to eradicate them from stock of every kind. Animals displaying these faults should not be used for breeding.

DEAFNESS
Swedish and Dutch scientists have advanced a theory, as yet unconfirmed, that deafness in Dalmatians may be genetically dominant. How then can we account for the numerous matings of two animals or normal hearing which produce deaf puppies in the normal ratio of the recessive? If deafness were dominant, one at any rate of the parents ought to have been deaf and we cannot suppose that all deafness is so slight as to be unidentifiable.

The opinions of established breeders would provide useful evidence. Until more facts are available we should continue to control deafness by never breeding from a deaf animal, destroying all deaf puppies and, a counsel of perfection, never breeding from an animal which has produced deaf puppies.

The superb animal which is a carrier is a problem. It will transmit deafness to half its progeny which are identifiable only by test-mating.

The first illustration shall be that of two Dalmatian parents each possessing a gene pair consisting of one dominant gene for hearing and one recessive gene for deafness. This mating is quite likely to occur in Dalmatians for both animals will have perfect hearing. A mating involving one deaf parent is unlikely to occur, for no responsible breeder would allow such a mating, or retain a deaf Dalmatian.

The parents in this particular case are hybrids for the character of hearing, as the word hybrid is used genetically, for their gene pairs control characters which are dissimilar and opposed to each other. Each carries the gene for deafness masked by its opposed dominant, the gene for hearing. They are therefore 'carriers'.

As we have seen, the gene pairs divide before fertilization. They can recombine in the fertilized egg in three different ways, resulting in three genetic types, though two of these present no external and observable differences.

Since the genetic pattern is not always reflected in the observable characters, we must here introduce two new words: Phenotype, the observable appearance, the Genotype, the hereditary pattern.

The genes we are considering therefore present three genotypes, but only two phenotypes.

The first way in which the two genes can combine is that two dominant genes form the new gene pair. The puppy which possesses this combination will hear, and it will not be able to pass on a gene for deafness to any of its progeny for it does not possess one. Its phenotype and genotype are identical.

In the second type of gene combination, two recessive genes for deafness will come together. The puppy with these will be deaf and will pass on the gene for deafness to all its progeny for it does not possess the gene for hearing. In this case also phenotype and genotype are identical.

The third type is that which has a gene pair like the parents, consisting of one dominant and one recessive gene. Owing to the presence of the dominant gene for hearing, this puppy will hear, but will pass on its recessive gene for deafness to half its progeny. In this case the phenotype and genotype are dissimilar, the puppy is a genetic hybrid for hearing.

It will be obvious that though three genetic types arise from such a mating, two are indistinguishable from each other (except by the test of their progeny).

When large numbers of litters are concerned, the average proportions expected of these types are as follows:

Out of an average of four puppies, one will have the double dominant gene pair for hearing, one will have the double recessive gene pair for deafness, two will have one gene for hearing and one for deafness in their gene pairs.

Three therefore out of the four will hear, though two of the three will be hybrids; one will be deaf.

No average figures are valid when small numbers are concerned. The classical example to illustrate this is that of tossing a coin. If tossed ten times, heads (or tails) could turn up ten times without creating undue surprise. Tossed ten thousand times, the proportions would be about equal.

Dominant genes and their opposed recessive partners are indicated genetically by using the capital letter of an appropriate word for the dominant member, and the small (lower case) letter for the recessive. Thus the pair for hearing would be H and h.

COAT COLOUR IN DALMATIANS

The permitted coat colours in the Dalmatian are black and brown (liver) and it has been stated by geneticists writing on the subject of canine coat colour that black is always dominant to liver; that, in fact, these two colours are an example of the classic dominant-recessive relationship already described. Marca Burns, in her most interesting and useful book *The Genetics of the Dog*, agrees with this statement. She has summarized the views of the most important writers on canine genetics, in addition to giving her own, and writes:

'One gene about which all the workers seem to agree is the one which makes the dog produce chocolate pigment instead of black. This is recessive to its allelomorph (either of a gene pair at the same position on a chromosome pair) which, when present, allows black pigment to be formed. These genes were named B (black) and b (chocolate) in 1914, and their relationship seems to be definite and simple, the gene b always behaving as a simple Mendelian recessive in B in every experiment that has been reported, in numerous breeds and their crosses.'

On the preceding page of her book she writes: 'It is a

curious fact that, although more scientific papers have been published on the subject of coat colour in dogs than on any other aspect of canine genetics, and despite the ease of observing and recording coat colour, yet the subject remains full of uncertainties and contradictions.'

I know of a number of matings which have produced puppies the coat colour of which appear to form an exception to this apparently universal rule, in fact they are one of the contradictions mentioned by Miss Burns. Liver mated to liver has produced black puppies; in all these cases I know the breeders well and nearly all the animals concerned. Something of the same kind has been recorded in both Pointers and Poodles.

An English geneticist to whom I have reported the occurrences has been most reluctant to accept them.

The opinion given is that in every case the result is due to mis-mating, or alternatively to a mutation. The latter cannot possibly explain the reversals which have occurred in two matings between the same animals. The former I do not believe. In several cases no other dogs were available; in every case the owners are most reliable and supervise matings themselves, in fact most do not employ kennel help.

Moreover there is no reason why these facts should not be as stated by breeders for no stigma attaches to the production of black puppies from two liver parents. The final example is of a liver dog (H) and a liver bitch (G) owned by sisters living some distance apart. The one took her liver dog to the sister who owned the bitch and no other Dalmatian existed for miles round her home. There was no possibility of any mis-mating, and both sisters were well-known and highly responsible people.

I submitted these findings to the well-known American geneticist Dr Clarence Little, who has been working on coat colour in dogs for nearly fifty years. He wrote back at length and I quote the relevant part of his reply: 'There seems no doubt that you have shown that there are two genetic types of colour described as "liver" in Dalmatians. The problem therefore becomes one of attempting by analogy to suggest types of colour resembling liver in appearance but differing from it genetically.'

A summary of the matings mentioned may be useful.

Bitch		Dog	Result
liver A	X	liver B	all black litter
liver A	X	liver C	all liver litter
liver D	X	liver B	all black litter
liver D	X	liver B	all black litter
Black (several)	X	liver B	mixed litters
liver E	X	liver F	all black litter
liver G	X	liver H	all black litter
liver G	X	liver H	all liver litter

It will be noticed that in the last mating between two liver dogs which had previously produced an all black litter, an all liver litter was born.

The production of mixed black and liver litters is normal, provided the black partner is the hybrid already mentioned which possesses one gene for black and one for liver. Similarly the all liver litter from two liver parents conforms with the accepted theory, though the fact that they could also produce an all black litter would not confirm this. I find it impossible to believe that all these results are due to mismatings.

Experts are of course liable to be wedded to their theories and reluctant to abandon them, even in face of what would appear to be good evidence. No doubt an occasion will arise when evidence will be provided that cannot be dismissed as lightly as this has been.

In the meantime I remain entirely convinced that in Dalmatians at any rate, and probably in Pointers and Poodles, two differing genetic combinations will be found to be responsible for what we call liver, as Dr Little has suggested.

Lemon. The colour we call lemon, a yellowish pale fawn, occurs occasionally; it has not, as far as I know, been mentioned by geneticists except by the American writer

Leon Whitney in *How to breed Dogs*. When discussing coat colour in Dalmatians he writes: 'One breeder told me of having seen lemon-spotted dogs, he knew nothing of their breeding.' But writing in the same book on coat colour in Pointers, Whitney, quoting from Clarence Little, writes: 'It is well known to breeders of dogs that yellows are of two very different types. This holds true in the case of Pointers. One type is a bright vivid yellow with *dark eyes and black nose*. The other type is duller and often lighter yellow with *pinkish-brown nose* and *light eyes*.'

The fact that this refers to Pointers may be of some significance to our breed, for there were undoubted Pointer crosses towards the end of the last century when Dalmatians were required to be as much like Pointers as possible.

It would be extremely interesting to know whether lemon as a colour had occurred in Dalmatian spotting before that time. I have not seen the colour mentioned in any of the books on dogs in my possession. Even hound crosses are quite likely to have been made in the long history of the breed. This seems a reasonable explanation of lemon spotting, an entity in itself in Dalmatians but not an accepted colour.

Breeders of today do not always realize that until comparatively recently few breeds could have been described as entirely pure-bred. Breeders of the more distant past were apt to mate their bitches, in nearly every case workers, to any dog of a breed likely to be able to introduce a desired quality into their stock. Pedigrees were few and registrations were non-existent. Cross breeding likely to make valuable contributions to working ability was the order of the day.

Tricolouration. This is stated in the standard to be a fault. It is the occurrence of black and liver spots on the same Dalmatian already mentioned in Chapter 3.

Whereas it was formerly believed to be caused by the mixing of black and liver blood, it is now thought to be due to a separate gene for mixed colouration, and this seems to be borne out by its incidence. Genetically speaking this theory involves the substitution of a modifying gene constituting a different pattern of inheritance, for one of the B or b genes affecting the colour of Dalmatian spotting.

Tricoloured dogs may have a large number of liver spots among the black, widely distributed over the body, head, and limbs. The liver spotting may be confined to the inside of the legs, the traditional area in all breeds where brown markings are likely to occur. Exceptionally only one or two spots are involved. I have myself never seen a liver-spotted Dalmatian with black spots, the condition is usually found in the black-spotted variety.

True tricolouration is usually found as soon as the spots appear in early puppyhood. Occasionally dogs are met with which develop liver marking only later, by about the end of the first year.

Tricolouration is technically a fault of decoration, decreed to be a fault fairly late in the history of the breed. Until the end of the nineteenth century it was looked upon as an attraction, adding variety to the decoration and not to be condemned.

Since all our present-day Dalmatians are descended from these animals it is only to be expected that this fault should occur from time to time.

Bronzing and Blackening. Another feature not uncommon in Dalmatians, and especially, I have noticed, in those with mixed black and liver blood, is the bronzing which may occur at certain stages of the coat. Normally black dogs develop a rustiness of some black spots giving them a brownish appearance. If the spots are examined it will be seen that the tips of the hairs only are affected, the base remains black. It would appear to be a type of fading, possibly due to the mixed blood, which could lend substance to the view that black is not always completely dominant to liver. The spots affected are not always the same.

In liver dogs a change also occurs. The liver colour darkens to such an extent that on casual inspection one would take the dog to be a poor black, only the ears show liver colour. The true colour returns, as black does in the case of the black dog, when the new coat is complete.

Patches. These are areas of solid colour *present at birth* when no other pigment in the coat is developed, for the spots begin to make their appearance only at about two weeks of age.

The hair on patches is uniformly dense in colour, without a single white hair, a few of which are often seen in Dalmatians' spots. Hair on patches seems to be a softer texture than normal.

Patches can occur anywhere on the body, but are probably most often seen on the head, involving one or both ears, the pigment showing a pattern rather like that of the typical Fox-terrier marking. A collection of spots which have run together does not constitute a patch.

Patched puppies should be put down, they should not be sold or bred from. Patching is without doubt hereditary, though, like many other aspects of coat colour in Dalmatians, it has not been investigated.

TOXOCARA CANIS
The official name of the most common type of roundworm, is known to all dog breeders. This worm is a parasite of the young puppy which is infected by larvae while still within the uterus of the bitch. The worms reach the bitch's intestine within about three days of birth; they grow and become mature about the ninth day of life and start producing eggs when the pup has reached the age of about two months.

The eggs pass out in the faeces and the life cycle then depends on the type of animal swallowing an infected egg; if this is a pup under three weeks of age the larvae hatch from the eggs in the intestine and migrate through the bowel wall to reach the liver. From here they are carried by the bloodstream to the lungs from which they are coughed up and swallowed, thus reaching the gut again, where they become mature worms.

If the dog is over three weeks old the larvae pass into various body tissues where they remain dormant. The eggs may be swallowed by a mouse or a rat, in which case the larvae hatch out and migrate, to remain dormant until the rodent, in turn is eaten by a dog, when adult worms may infest the dog's intestine.

The egg may be swallowed by a child and, as in the mouse, the larvae again hatch and migrate into the body tissues, occasionally causing severe damage when they come to rest in vital organs, especially the eye. For this reason alone, children should not be allowed to play, or even come into close contact with untreated puppies and should not allow dogs of any age to lick their faces. Adult toxocara worms disappear from the intestine of a dog over twelve months of age.

(With acknowledgements to the unknown author and the Animal Health Trust).

CRYPTORCHIDISM

A cryptorchid dog is one in which either or both testicles are absent from the scrotum. The word does not describe a dog in which one or both testicles are absent from the body. Therefore the terms as commonly used, cryptorchid and monorchid, are anatomically incorrect.

One or both testicles may be retained within the abdomen, in the kidney region where they take origin in pre-natal life, lower down in the abdomen, or in the inguinal canal. If one testicle is present in the scrotum and the other retained, the dog is a one-sided or unilateral cryptorchid, if both are retained the dog is a double, or bilateral cryptorchid.

A bilateral cryptorchid dog is sterile, the higher temperature within the abdomen reacting unfavourably on the sperms manufactured in the testicle.

Moreover there is a tendency for malignant changes to take place in an undescended testicle, in dogs as in humans. The normal disposition of the animal often changes, probably by the changes in normal sex hormones made in the testicles.

Bilateral cryptorchids are, as already mentioned, sterile. Unilateral cryptorchids are able to sire normal litters, though one or two of the few Dalmatians suffering from this defect have not been very fertile sires. It seems certain that bitches can carry the gene for the defect, though for obvious reasons they cannot display it. The exact method of its inheritance has not yet been firmly established and views on the question differ.

Cryptorchids of either variety are banned from the show-ring here as in other countries. We have as yet no ban on breeding from them. On general principles any factor which tends to diminish fertility, or could do so, is a potential danger to the breed in which it occurs. Our modern dogs have to contend with many conditions which may react unfavourably on reproduction, for instance mass production with consequent overcrowding and poor nutrition, show-ring fashions which in some breeds have a directly bad effect on reproduction, the generally unnatural life of many dogs today, confined in small spaces, with no opportunities for adequate bodily development, surely these are enough without adding even more which contribute to lack of fertility.

As far as Dalmatians are concerned, we have very few dogs which are not entire. Our puppies normally show evidence of testicles soon after birth, by slight swellings on the scrotal sac on both sides which develop into normal testicles in the usual position fairly rapidly.

HIP DYSPLASIA

Although given a name only fairly recently, this condition must have been present for a long time in certain breeds, described as 'lameness'. Dalmatians fortunately are little affected by it so far, though one or two cases are known. Possibly there are others which have not been diagnosed because their owners have not thought the lameness to be of any great consequence or perhaps have not faced the facts.

Investigation has shown that, although the exact method of inheritance is not yet certain, it is probable that a number of genes are involved and that inheritance is dominant in character. These are the conclusions of Helen Hein, B.V.M.S.,

M.R.C.V.S., who is actively engaged in research on this condition.

Two methods, complementary to each other, exist for the diagnosis of hip dysplasia. One is the use of Radiography, the picture taken and the result studied by experts in this particular field. The other is by the occurrence of outward signs of the disease. Changes occur in the bones which form the hip-joint, already described in Chapter 5. The deep socket becomes flattened and more shallow, the round head of the femur also flattens and the fit between ball and socket becomes progressively worse, eventually there may be complete dislocation of one or both hips. All stability is lost in the joints involved. Some cases may be so severe that the afflicted dogs walk carrying their hind legs in the air. Films of this condition have been made.

In the early stages, sometimes seen at about five months of age, often not until later, puppies become disinclined for exercise and certain movements involving the hip-joint. They tend to sit about and dislike being disturbed. The gait may become swaying, in severe cases a clicking noise is heard in the hip-joint. Dalmatians so far have been fortunate in that very few cases of hip dysplasia are known. Any unexplained persistent lameness should be promptly referred to a veterinary surgeon who has both especial knowledge of the condition and can take X-rays and interpret them with expert knowledge.

If this is done, and no animal were bred from which had any sign of this defect, either radiological or visible, we should avoid any spread from the small number we now have of affected dogs.

As Miss Hein says: 'As far as breeding stock is concerned, any animal showing radiographic signs of this condition should never be used for breeding. If this precaution is observed, genetic factors for normal hip-joints will be selected while those associated with the defect should automatically be discarded.'

Hip dysplasia does not appear to be actively painful though the disability is extreme in advanced cases. The condition has long been known in man as 'Congenital Dislocation of the Hip'.

As far as we know, Dalmatians do not suffer from many hereditary diseases known in dogs. Progressive Retinal Atrophy (night blindness) and slipping patella are unknown.

In fact Dalmatian anatomy in the sound animal could hardly be better suited to normal activity and the fulfilment of all bodily functions.

13

The Dalmatian in Sickness

The object of this chapter is to mention briefly the various categories of disease to which the Dalmatian, in common with other breeds, may fall a victim, with a mention of the preventive measures which can be taken in cases where these exist; to draw attention to the new hazards to which modern farming methods of pest and weed destruction now expose our dogs; and to give a little practical advice on some of the minor ills in which the veterinary surgeon is called in late if at all.

An account of all diseases and their treatment is outside the scope of this book and is in any case the province of the veterinary surgeon.

We must begin by stating that the Dalmatian is among the healthiest and hardiest of breeds. His structure is sturdy and all that could be desired from the point of view of fitness for the normal functions of living. His stamina is still that of his forbears which followed the coaches and carriages of the past for many miles. His aptitude for this traditonal task has not forsaken him and some fortunate Dalmatians still enjoy their former work.

The Dalmatian, however, is not immune from the diseases which can attack the healthiest dog as they can the healthiest man.

Fortunately methods are now available which can prevent or mitigate the killing infections of both man and dog. For example, we inoculate our dogs against distemper, canine virus hepatitis, and leptospiral jaundice; we inoculate our children against smallpox, diphtheria, and poliomyelitis.

The refusal of such protection to children and dogs seems to me a crime.

Resistance to disease can be strengthened by the choice of

sound healthy stock for breeding, good rearing and management of puppies and young stock, a normal healthy life, and the protection given against infections by inoculation. Constant observation, as a normal routine, ensures that any early signs of illness shall not be overlooked.

This observation becomes automatic, and the intimate knowledge thus gained of a healthy dog enables the owner to detect the smallest abnormalities of appearance or behaviour.

Before dealing with conditions which affect the animal directly, there is one which affects newly born puppies indirectly, through their dam, and it is in a category of its own in this respect.

FADING PUPPIES

The history of this condition is as follows: An apparently healthy bitch gives birth to an apparently healthy litter and for a day or two all seems well. Then, for no apparent reason, some or all of the puppies cease to thrive. They are cold and lethargic, refuse to feed, cry constantly and feebly, become rapidly weaker, and, without treatment, they die in the course of a day or two.

This is an emergency which calls for immediate veterinary treatment which may be successful if given in time.

The causes are various, we already know some, probably more will be discovered. The first to be described some twenty years ago was infection of the dam by Beta Haemolytic Streptococcus, the toxins of which probably passed from her blood to that of the unborn whelps through the placental circulation. No actual streptococcus was found in the tissues of puppies dying from this cause.

Since then other causes have been discovered, notably that of a previous infection of the dam by canine virus hepatitis. The Canine Section of the Animal Health Trust was responsible for this research. In this case the blood of the dam of puppies dying from this cause will show evidence of a past attack and this evidence may last for a year or more after an attack.

Incompatibility of blood groups may also be a cause of

fading puppies (this occurs also in human infants and such cases are now treated by a complete change of the entire blood of the baby). Recent research, however, shows that the symptoms of this condition are not identical with those of 'fading'.

Briefly, incompatibility of blood groups is a condition in which the blood corpuscles of one group are clotted by the liquid serum of another group to form solid masses, a condition incompatible with life.

Poor management also contributes to fading puppies by undermining the natural resistance which is not fully developed at this tender age.

Puppy fading is an emergency in which only prompt treatment by the veterinary surgeon offers any chance of success.

BACTERIAL AND VIRUS INFECTIONS

These probably constitute the greatest threat to dogs. Fortunately a number can be controlled by preventive vaccination. Distemper in its varying forms is one of these, it includes the so-called hard pad disease; canine virus hepatitis is another; leptospiral jaundice, a form of rapidly fatal jaundice transmitted both to humans and dogs by contamination by the urine of infected rats, is yet another and a most dangerous infection, for jaundice does not occur early in the course of the illness and by the time it does treatment may be too late.

Inoculation against these three serious infections can now be combined in a single dose and should be routine treatment for all puppies, followed later by a booster injection.

Canicola fever is another complaint which affects dogs and humans alone, it is due to the same type of organism as leptospiral jaundice. It is transmitted by the urine of an infected dog. Canicola attacks the kidneys and some of the nephritis common in elderly dogs is thought to be due to an attack of this disease in early life, possibly so slight as to have been unrecognized.

The product Gamahtine, isolated by the research workers of the Canine Health Centre of the Animal Health Trust some years ago and still prepared by them for marketing by one of the most respected firms, consists of the small fraction of the blood serum which contains the protective substances manufactured by the animal body itself in response to infection. Each of these substances, called 'antibodies', is specific for each infecting organism. Gamahtine is in constant use, not only in veterinary but in human medical practice.

The earliest signs of infection of any kind are much the same. It is a safe rule to call in the veterinary surgeon to any Dalmatian which persistently refuses food and shows one or more of the following signs: a temperature of 103°F. or over with a rapid pulse rate, lethargy in an otherwise lively dog, diarrhoea or vomiting or both, with a progressive rise in temperature taken four-hourly. This should be done in the rectum and a short clinical thermometer gives the least chance of breaking. It should be inserted gently into the rectum in a forward direction for about an inch and held there for a full minute.

Most Dalmatians do not resent this, but any serious resistance calls for help in holding the dog.

It cannot be too much emphasized that early diagnosis and treatment in any case of serious infection is urgent and no delay should be caused by experiments with aspirin or any other medicament.

It is not always realized that dogs suffer from many of our human diseases as well as those specifically their own. Dalmatians can have pneumonia, various forms of heart disease, diseases of the kidneys, cancer in all its forms. Diabetes is known though uncommon, and the terminal illness of many old dogs is the type of chronic nephritis so well known in humans, in which the kidneys gradually fail and eventually cease to function altogether, leading to uraemia, coma, and death.

This type of kidney trouble may be suspected when a middle-aged or elderly dog begins to lose weight and condition, and frequently passes large quantities of pale urine. An analysis of this and an estimation of the dog's blood urea will settle the diagnosis.

The kidney and bladder stones which may occur in Dalmatians show different signs. They commonly occur in younger dogs, may come on suddenly with acute pain if a stone is lodged in the ureter (the tube which conducts urine from kidney to bladder), or in the urethra (the shorter tube from bladder to the exterior). Kidney stones themselves can cause a different type of pain. Blood is often passed with the urine and occasionally also a kind of brownish sand, which consists of the debris of stones. The dog's hind action is often affected, becoming stiff.

Medical treatment can usually relieve the condition for a time unless a stone is actually impacted in the urinary tract. Operation can remove such a stone or one elsewhere, but it seems doubtful in the dog's interest whether it should be imposed when permanent cure cannot be certain.

As already mentioned, this condition seems to run in families, suggesting an hereditary factor, not for excess uric acid which is believed to be common to all Dalmatians, but for the ability to cope with it, absent in those animals which are actively afflicted with these stones.

Pneumonia may be suspected if the dog has a hard cough, a high temperature, and a very rapid rate of breathing with obvious signs of illness.

Heart conditions are suggested by breathlessness on any exertion, dropsy, and possibly a blue tinge in the lining membrane of the mouth.

Cancer is common in older dogs, though the type which affects bone is often found in youth. This disease includes also the various forms of cancer of the blood, the leukaemias, which may be suspected when glands all over the body enlarge but are not painful. Glands enlarge in septic conditions, but are then exceedingly tender.

Most types of cancer are painless in their earlier stages, and there may be nothing to draw attention to them until the disease is far advanced. The question as to whether operation in such cases is kind or wise has once more to be considered.

Tuberculosis is not common in dogs but cases are known. A bitch of my own presented a classical case of tuberculosis of the spine nine months after the beginning of the last war, when only knacker's meat was available for dogs. I foolishly thought that it could safely be given raw for a day or two, if I looked carefully for any tuberculous glands and removed them. I was wrong, and since then I have always recommended careful and thorough cooking of knacker's meat if this has to be given.

This case was an example of the bovine type of tubercle. I have not heard of any lung tubercle in dogs, though it probably exists.

SKIN TROUBLES

Dalmatians suffer comparatively little from these; their short coats, which they keep clean by licking, are easily managed and a bath is not a major operation for a Dalmatian.

Skin parasites of various kinds, however, do exist and occasionally our breed is afflicted with them. Fleas can occur in summer.

They are not difficult to catch, for they walk instead of hopping as in the human variety. Fleas do not breed on the dog, they lay their eggs in suitable cracks in woodwork or floor. They are the host of the tapeworm and should be entirely banished if only for this reason. A regular dusting with Pulvex or some other preparation once or twice weekly if necessary will destroy fleas and keep them away.

Lice on the other hand are a different class of pest. They are rarely seen on healthy well-cared for dogs. They breed on the dog and the eggs, called nits, are attached firmly to the dog's hairs. The eggs are not killed by the usual antiseptic preparations and must be destroyed after hatching, making necessary a succession of baths or applications in an infested dog. A veterinary surgeon should be consulted, for the newer and more effective preparations must be used with caution and strictly according to instructions.

Ticks. Dalmatians, like most other dogs, occasionally pick up ticks if they are country dogs, and especially if they live in sheep country. The short coats of our dogs make ticks easy to see, they form small lumps on the skin. The hair growing at that point is staring, and if the ticks are gorged with blood they can be as large as a small cherry and impossible to miss. They should not be pulled off or the head will be left behind which gives rise to a nasty intractable sore. A drop or two of turpentine, or I should think, methylated spirit, applied to the tick causes it to fall off intact.

Harvest Mites. These pests are common in country districts from July to September and they can be as much of a nuisance to dogs as they are to humans. They are minute burrowing mites crab-like in shape, and though bright red, so small as to be practically invisible. They attack the skin, usually most where two skin surfaces touch each other. Common sites to be attacked in the dog are between the toes, under the arms, and inside the legs where the hair is at its minimum. Flowers of sulphur dusted lightly once a day on affected areas will usually prevent this insect from burrowing, and if present will destroy it. Sulphur should be used with discretion or the harvest-mite irritation may be exchanged for a sulphur dermatitis.

And now we come to two more serious skin parasites, those of the two varieties of mange.

Sarcoptic Mange (or Scabies). This is also due to a burrowing parasite and causes intense irritation, with constant scratching and a pronounced mousy smell. Infection is likely to follow the sores made by scratching the bare areas where the parasite has lodged. This skin disease is communicated from dog to man and from man to dog. Easy methods of diagnosis are available to the veterinary surgeon, treatment is successful and not prolonged.

Demodectic Mange (or Follicular Mange) is a more serious and difficult condition. It affects in the main young dogs, and is caused by a parasite which lives in the roots of the hair (the hair follicles), and is thus more difficult to reach by local treatment.

Irritation and scratching are less than in the other variety, but the mousy smell is also present. Bare patches of skin develop, which may become thickened and scaly.

In contrast to scabies this type of mange is not very contagious.

Follicular Mange used to be considered as practically incurable. Modern research has provided methods of cure which have been successful in many cases.

The veterinary surgeon is able to diagnose both types of mange by skin scrapings, and he should be consulted in any skin condition, for these are notoriously difficult to treat when once fully established.

Ringworm. This is caused by several types of fungus which affect the skin and form small round, almost bald, areas with a few broken hairs growing in the bare places. This fungus also invades the roots of the hair. There is very little scratching, but the condition is highly contagious, from man to dog or the reverse. Veterinary surgeons can diagnose and treat ringworm successfully.

And now we come to another skin condition probably more common than any yet mentioned, and this is *Eczema*, of which there are two varieties, the one a dry scaly eruption, the other and the more common, a moist type with much exudation from the affected areas. Moist eczema comes on with great rapidity and in a few hours a normal piece of skin can be swollen, shiny, moist, and hairless. Thirty years ago this used to be treated with tar lotions and other remedies and the course of the disease was prolonged. Since the discovery of the part played by histamine in skin allergies the picture has changed and a few doses of an anti-histamine preparation usually cures moist eczema in the course of a very few days; the cure is quite spectacular.

Dogs are susceptible to substances which release histamine into the tissues just as humans are, and I shall never forget an experience of my own nearly thirty years ago, and before we knew of the existence of histamine. I was taking my dogs for a walk along the ancient grass track which ran past our house when I noticed one lagging behind, and when I looked I saw his face and head swelling up as I watched; within a few moments he dropped unconscious.

I was alone and some way from home, but I knew that my small staff would be going to church along this track shortly and when they came I sent them home with the other dogs and waited until my husband came along with a wheelbarrow, into which we lifted the still-unconscious dog, took him home, and wrapped him in a blanket before a fire. Fortunately he regained consciousness very soon, and within a few hours was perfectly normal. What he had absorbed we never knew.

I often think how very fortunate we are today, thanks to the devoted efforts of those whose lifework is the investigation of new drugs and their application.

Many of the allergy-producing substances are now well-known, but their action occurs only with susceptible people. The discovery of the anti-histamine drugs has revolutionized the treatment of these extremely dangerous allergies.

INTERNAL PARASITES

Fortunately we in England are free from some of the dangerous parasites which may afflict dogs in some other parts of the world. The roundworm (already dealt with) and the tapeworm are the most common here.

The tapeworm needs an intermediate host in which to pass part of its life cycle. The rabbit and the flea perform this function. The mature tapeworm or series of tapeworms, for each section is complete in itself as far as reproduction goes, has a head which attaches itself to the lining of the bowel by hooks. Flat whitish segments, each not unlike a small piece of tape, develop behind this head, one behind the other, the smallest being nearest to the head, the largest at the tail end, eventually being passed through the anus in a mature condition. Shed on grass, their eggs, the product of the male and female elements contained in each segment, may be eaten by the intermediate host, the rabbit or flea, in which they form cysts in the tissues within which a number of new heads develop and start the cycle again.

Dried tapeworm segments may sometimes be seen sticking to the anus of infected dogs, often noticeable in those which run the streets or village lanes. They look rather like grains of rice. It is important to get rid of a tapeworm and the veterinary surgeon should be consulted, for the most effective drugs, as already mentioned, are not sold over the counter.

It is especially important to observe the results of the drug for if the head is left behind another series of segments will grow from it. The dog should be watched until it has produced the worm, which may be broken up into several lengths or may be intact. The worm should be picked up with two sticks and allowed to float in water, the head can then be seen, with a magnifying glass if necessary, at the smallest end; it is round, and usually rather smaller than a pin head. If this is clearly identified the worm has been entirely expelled. Some modern remedies dissolve the worm, in which case nothing will be seen.

POISONS

Many more dangerous preparations are in common use today than ever before, and among the most dangerous are those over which dog owners have no control.

We can at least be sure that in our own houses and kennels dogs can come to no harm and we can ensure this as far as chemical substances are concerned by keeping anything dangerous out of their reach.

The only way in which we can be safe is a rigid routine by which every substance is labelled, has its own place in a cupboard which can be firmly closed or locked, and is returned to that place immediately after use. Drugs are not the only dangers, cleaning fluids, oven cleaners (often caustic soda), ammonia, strong acids, even detergents, can do great, even if not fatal, harm. Only when such a routine is established, for a kennel staff as well as for a single owner, can ease of mind on this point be assured.

Gas can be dangerous. At the time when gas pressure was often reduced at night, I know of an owner who had been cooking late. She forgot something left in the oven on a comparatively low heat and went to bed leaving three dogs to sleep in the kitchen. Reduced pressure caused the gas to go out, and it came on in the early morning at more pressure. She found two dead dogs when she came down and one hardly alive. Eternal vigilance is certainly the price of safety in small matters as in great.

Apart from domestic hazards many poisonous substances

are used in agriculture and in weed destruction today. Treatment of seed corn with pest-destroying chemicals has undoubtedly caused the death of many birds and of other creatures who ate the bodies. In my own area wholesale casualties of pigeons were followed by the deaths of many foxes and no doubt other less harmful animals, among which dogs might easily be included.

Not only pigeons suffered; countless useful birds which keep down insect pests lose their lives even today. Once the balance of nature has been disturbed the end result may be disastrous. Apart from this, surely we have not yet reached the point at which nothing beautiful can be allowed to survive unless for some purely utilitarian aim.

The weedkillers used today wholesale along verges and in fields are also dangerous, some contain arsenic which may be fatal and which causes intense pain to any animal which eats contaminated grass. I know of one such fatal case in my own neighbourhood. A poison used extensively in killing rats is also a danger to dogs. This is Warfarin. It is cumulative in effect. A single dose causes little harm, repeated doses affect clotting of the blood, and may cause sudden death during any great exertion. This was discovered by the Animal Health Trust Canine section, working on the death of greyhounds which dropped dead while racing. Warfarin is used in the most lighthearted way by many ill-informed country people and I have been assured repeatedly that it is perfectly harmless to everything but rats.

It is not uncommon, though strictly illegal, to lay food in the open baited with strychnine to destroy foxes. A very nice puppy I sold years ago picked up a piece of rabbit so treated, and she died in great agony. A post-mortem examination proved the cause and the police made enquiries but the culprit was never discovered.

A number of dangerous modern pesticides have been banned since their tragic effect on wild life and the environment became apparent, but there is no guarantee that small quantities left over will not be used by careless or unscrupulous people. Everyone should be wary of substances which are advertised as 'harmless to pets and children' unless the chemical analysis can be thoroughly understood.

Pain cannot be measured by time, as anyone knows who has experienced it in its acutest form, but absence of pain does not mean that a dog is not suffering, and this brings me to my final subject.

THE OLD DALMATIAN
We have discussed general management of the elderly Dalmatian. We come now to the dog in advanced old age.

Dalmatians live comparatively long lives, often reaching thirteen or even fourteen years of age, and few die earlier than ten or eleven, apart from specific diseases. But there comes a time in the life of every old dog, when he begins to fail, without showing any signs of a definite trouble, or any pain. But a feeling of weariness, lassitude, and illness, a lack of interest in life and all the doggy pleasures, can be present in the absence of any pain, for pain is not the sole criterion of distress.

We can spare our old friends this long-drawn-out misery, and if we really love them we do so, and when this moment comes we recognize it almost instinctively.

Veterinary surgeons are kindly humane people and the painless method of destruction now possible can be used so easily and gently that the dog knows nothing at all, often not even feeling the prick of the needle.

May I suggest to those who love their Dalmatians that their dogs should not be taken or sent to the veterinary surgeon but should be allowed to die in their own home with their owner there to the last. This is the final service we can render to our old friends.

POST-WAR DALMATIAN
REGISTRATIONS

1946	809	1966	1911
1947	745	1967	2348
1948	761	1968	3218
1949	753	1969	2916
1950	538	1970	2752
1951	490	1971	2049
1952	476	1972	2291
1953	497	1973	2161
1954	397	1974	2044
1955	543	1975	1193
1956	579	1976	486
1957	656	1977	302
1958	766	1978	750
1959	791	1979	974
1960	906	1980	937
1961	1112	1981	745
1962	1438	1982	699
1963	1549	1983	756
1964	1658	1984	681
1965	1714		

DALMATIAN CLUBS
and their Secretaries

The British Dalmatian Club
    Mrs J. Curtis, 'Sydon', 4 Vicarage Road, Silsoe, Bedford.
The North of England Dalmatian Club
    Mrs D. McKay, Blandford Cottage, Anchorage Avenue, Hundred End, Hesketh Bank, Lancashire.
The Dalmatian Club of Scotland
    Mrs C. Whyte, 'Mansfield', Gleve Road, Kilbirnie, Ayrshire.
The All-Ireland Dalmatian Club
    Mr J. P. Cunningham, 123 Upper Leesen Street, Dublin.
CANADA
    Mrs Penny Paul, 37 St James Court, Leamington, Ontario.
FINLAND
Dalmatinerna R. Y.
    Pertti Kiho, 10160 Dergerby UL.
FRANCE
Dalmatien Club Français
    Mme E. Garaix, 8 Avenue Larcher, Chatou 78400.
GERMANY
Deutscher Dalmatiner Club von 1920 E. V.
    Dipl. Ing. A. Ronneburg, Poppenweiler Strasse 16, 7142 Marbach/Neckar.
SWITZERLAND
Schweiz-Dalmatiner Club
    Mrs E. Luisier, 95 Route de Suisse, 1290 Nersoix.
BELGIUM
Belgische v. Dalmatische Honden
    Mrs M. Huylebroek-Ongers, Flet Nenneke 12, 2130 Brasschaast.
NETHERLANDS
Nederlandse Club v. Dalmatische Honden

Mrs A. Morgans-Huisman, Spoorstraat 33, 3862 AC Nÿkerk.

SWEDEN
Svenska Dalmatiner-Sallskepet
   Ann-Katrin Johansson, Fjardhundragt 40.753 37 Uppsala.

NORWAY
Norsk Dalmatiner Klubb
   Anne Grete Nordlund, 3220 Furnes.

HUNGARY
   Gyula Csekó Esq., 1141 Budapest, Szuglo u.106.

NEW ZEALAND
   Mrs K. Clayton, 35 Morrison Drive, Hobsonville.

AUSTRALIA
New South Wales
   Denise Mottek, 30 Spring Road, Kellyville 2153.
Victoria
   Mrs S. Angliss, 1 Coolamon Drive, Ocean Grove.
Queensland
   Mrs B. Deighton, 20 Oakfield Street, Mt Gravatt.
United States of America
Dalmatian Club of America, Inc., Mrs Christine Dyker, Route 1, Dickerson, MD 20753.
Dalmatian Club of Southern California, Mrs Maria Johnson, 5512 Danbury Place, Woodland Hills, California 91364.

OTHER REGIONAL CLUBS

Chicagoland Dalmatian Club
Davenport Dalmatian Club
Greater Washington Dal Club
Dalmatian Club of Las Vegas
Greater Pittsburgh Dalmatian Club
Dalmatian Club of Greater St Louis
Dalmatian Club of Southern New England
Dalmatian Organization of Houston
Western Reserve Dalmatian Club
Dal Club of Greater New York
Detroit Dalmatian Club

Greater Sacramento Dalmatian Club
Mount Hood Dal Club
Dalmatian Club of Greater Phoenix
Puget Sound Dalmatian Club
Dalmatian Club of Greater Atlanta

There are Dalmatians also in the Argentine, Denmark, Italy, Mexico, Poland, Portugal, Spain and Yugoslavia.

POST-WAR DALMATIAN CHAMPIONS 1946–1974

Name	Sex	Sire	Dam	Owner	Breeder	Date of Birth
1946						
Ch. Tantivvey Naomi	B	Ch. George of the River	Patrician Maid	Miss I. B. Clay	Miss I. B. Clay	4.6.42
1947						
Ch. Muggins Moses	D	Merrie Knight	Muggins Sally	Mrs Curphey	Mrs Curphey	15.8.44
Ch. Norseman of Welfield	D	Ch. George of the River	Patrician Maid	Mrs Bloomfield	Miss I. B. Clay	4.6.42
Ch. Turpins Shadow	D	Ch. Cabaret Copyright	Claudine the Woozle	E. W. Davies	E. W. Davies	25.8.40
Ch. Winnall Blackberry	B	Ch. Mahlib Jifft	Winnall Gay	R. Burr	Mrs Frankling	26.10.44
1948						
Ch. Ajax of Lornehill	D	Ch. Norseman of Welfield	Chloe of Welfield	Mrs Rogers	Mrs Rogers	25.1.46
Ch. Clef of the Carriageway	D	Ch. Norseman of Welfield	Chord of the Carriageway	Miss J. Whitton	Miss M. Coupe	3.10.45
Ch. Tobias of the Towpath	D	Ch. George of the River	Patrician Maid	Mrs Parker	Miss I. B. Clay	4.6.42
Ch. Cabaret Celeste	B	Cabaret Caretaker	Cabaret Goldcrest	Miss Monkhouse	Miss Monkhouse	30.5.46
Ch. Deanna of Dalmally	B	Ch. Mahlib Jifft	Cinderella of Dalmally	Mrs Buchanan	Mrs Buchanan	18.2.45

Name	Sex	Sire	Dam	Owner	Breeder	Date of Birth
Ch. Flora of the Wells	B	Spoleto of Kurnool	Domino's Daughter of Kurnool	Miss Barnes	Miss Barnes	3.2.45
Ch. Penny Parade	B	Kim of Welfield	Cabaret Commandant	Mrs Hoyle	Mrs Hoyle	10.4.44
Ch. Wellandvalley Lucy	B	Ch. Tobias of the Towpath	Jonstown Cordelia	Miss R. E. Hope	F. B. Frost	22.9.46
Ch. Winnall Elegance	B	Winnall Joker	Colonsay Rudder	Mrs Frankling	Mrs Rickwood	16.6.46
1949						
Ch. Ambala Bahadur of Bromholm	D	Winnall Joker	Delia of Dalmally	Mrs E. Allen	Mrs E. Allen	12.2.47
Ch. Ambala Sahib	D	Winnall Joker	Delia of Dalmally	Mrs E. Allen	Mrs E. Allen	12.2.47
Ch. Beau of Hollyroyde	D	Welfield Tracer	Dazzling Marjorie	Mrs Rawcliffe	Mrs Soo	2.6.47
Ch. Cabaret Cocoanut	D	Ch. Turpins Shadow	Cabaret Crystal	Miss Monkhouse	Miss Monkhouse	4.10.47
Ch. Colonsay Storm	D	Ch. Tobias of the Towpath	Colonsay Annie Mary	Miss Macfie	Mrs Stockman	10.9.48
Ch. Palfrey Trajan	D	Burnbrook Fergus	Kyogle Risk	Mrs M. Dru	Mrs J. M. Davis	30.12.45
Ch. Astwood Celia	B	Napoleon of Bidford	Astwood Cinders	J. C. Feast	Mrs L. Yeomans	18.6.46

198

	Sex	Sire	Dam			
Ch. Turnpike Tansy	B	Turnpike Proud Peter	Lyonsdown Bess	D. Stalker	Mrs H. Jones	7.11.46
Ch. Twink of the Towpath	B	Ch. Tobias of the Towpath	Toots of the Towpath	Mrs Parker	Mrs Parker	19.9.47
1950 Ch. Cabaret Conservative	D	Cabaret Maxroy	Aldham Rowena	Miss Monkhouse	T. Baines	19.8.47
Ch. Bo'sun Bobbie	D	Turnpike Proud Peter	Lyonsdown Bess	Mrs E. D. Macmillan	Mrs Jones	7.11.46
Ch. Raff of the Wells	D	Astwood Caesar	Domino's Daughter of Kurnool	Miss E. V. Barnes	Mrs B. H. Essam	3.3.48.
Ch. Colonsay Rolling Billow	B	Colonsay Black Cloud	Colonsay Rolling Seas	Mrs B. Usher	Miss Macfie	7.10.46
Ch. Postchaise Claudette	B	Ch. Turpins Shadow	Postchaise Betty	E. W. Davies	E. W. Davies	20.10.48
Ch. Tantivvey Godetia	B	Clef of the Carriageway	Tantivvey Genesta	T. B. Brinkworth	Miss I. B. Clay	9.6.48
1951 Ch. Lindally Briar	D	Ch. Muggins Moses	Ch. Winnall Blackberry	Mrs Polehampton	R. Burr	1.5.48
Ch. Tatters of the Towpath	D	Ch. Tobias of the Towpath	Jonstown Cordelia	Mrs Parker	Mrs Parker	16.4.49
Ch. Winnall Dazzler of Dalmally	D	Ch. Ambala Sahib	Ch. Deanna of Dalmally	Mrs Frankling	Mrs Buchanan	5.3.49

199

Name	Sex	Sire	Dam	Owner	Breeder	Date of Birth
Ch. Aldham Beauty	B	Mr Buttons of Dalmally	Shuna of Stonewall	Miss Smither	W. H. Blunt	14.6.47
Ch. Aldham Happy Reflection	B	Cabaret Maxroy	Aldham Rowena	Miss Smither	Major J. D. Atkinson	19.8.47
Ch. Baroness of Hatherley	B	Postchaise Clipper	Dallystar of Briariver	Mrs K. N. Rogers	Mrs M. W. Cooper	1.7.47
Ch. Bordette of Birch	B	Ch. Norseman of Welfield	Mytilene of Birch	L. Clarke	Mrs Nixey	30.5.47
Ch. Cabaret Charivaria	B	Ch. Cabaret Conservative	Lady Alma	Miss Monkhouse	F. Geary	21.8.49
1952						
Ch. Bramble of the Forest	D	Mesra Singlethought	Sidebones	Mrs Caldwell	Mrs Nixey	19.6.47
Ch. Cabaret Colonist	D	Ch. Cabaret Copyist	Arbour Black Beauty	Miss Monkhouse	C. Cotteril	24.4.49
Ch. Cabaret Copyist	D	Ch. Turpins Shadow	Cabaret Crystal	Miss Monkhouse	Miss Monkhouse	4.10.47
Ch. Cabaret Canasta	B	Ch. Cabaret Cocoanut	Chokka Wendy	Miss Monkhouse	Mrs E. Jubb	15.6.50
Ch. Clearspots Little Woman	B	Turnpike Bronze Idol	Megalene Lass	Mr and Mrs Essam	A. H. Burgwin	18.9.50

Name	Sex	Sire	Dam	Breeder	Owner	Date
Ch. Coolie of St Botoff	B	Bandit of St Botoff	Grindelford Bess	Capt. Fleeman	H. Blackburn	29.6.50
1953						
Ch. Cabaret Candid Consort	D	Ch. Cabaret Conservative	Cabaret Candace	Miss Monkhouse	Miss Monkhouse	8.11.51
Ch. Colonsay Charles Gibbs	D	Ch. Colonsay Storm	Colonsay Swashbuckler	Miss Macfie	Miss Macfie	14.5.50
Ch. Goworth Gambol	D	Goworth Colossus	Dalahope Diligence	{Mrs Wigglesworth Mrs Macdonald Smith}	Mrs Wakinshaw	21.1.51
Ch. Amaryllis of Widdington	B	Widdington Danilo of Dalmally	Widdington Peggotty	Mrs Hayman	Mrs Hayman	16.9.50
Ch. Iris of Fieldburcote	B	Winnall Joker	Tabitha of the Towpath	Miss Esme Watson	F. W. Ray	4.4.49
1954						
Ch. Horsemans Bobsworth	D	Ch. Bo'sun Bobbie	Horsemans Folly	Miss Heard	Miss Agate	6.4.51
Ch. Jobandit of St Botoff	D	Bandit of St Botoff	Rhapsody of Oudenarde	Capt. Fleeman	Miss de Mynn	18.9.52
Ch. Horsemans Shadow	B	Ch. Bo'sun Bobbie	Horsemans Folly	Miss Agate	Miss Agate	6.4.51
Ch. Lazaars Georgette	B	Ch. Bramble of the Forest	Knighton's Return	Mrs Caldwell	Mrs Caldwell	11.7.51
Ch. Winnall Bearscombe Betony	B	Ch. Winnall Dazzler of Dalmally	Lindally Aurora	Mrs Frankling	Mrs Rust	4.5.52

Name	Sex	Sire	Dam	Owner	Breeder	Date of Birth
1955						
Ch. Dalwynn Diehard	D	Ch. Cabaret Conservative	Ch. Bordette of Birch	L. Clarke	L. Clarke	16.11.51
Ch. Tweedle of the Towpath	D	Ch. Bramble of the Forest	Tulip of the Towpath	D. Stalker	Mrs P. Parker	15.2.52
Ch. Cabaret Coronel	B	Turnpike Bronze Idol	Cabaret Coppelia of Kurnool	Miss Monkhouse	Mrs Macdonald Smith	8.4.52
Ch. Jezebel of Fieldburcote	B	Tantivvey Donovan of Dalmally	Astwood Charmian	A. E. Johnson	Miss Esme Watson	21.8.51
Ch. Oubeck Tudor of the Towpath	B	Ch. Bramble of the Forest	Tilla of the Towpath	Mrs A. Bramley	Mrs P. Parker	22.2.52
1956						
Ch. Aldham George of Elberton	D	Ch. Horseman's Bobsworth	Hero of Redbraes	Miss V. Smither	Col. Scott-Lowe	8.8.53
Ch. Black Prince of Bellett	D	Tantivvey Castor of Bellett	Single Lady of Bellett	Mrs M. MacRobert	Mrs M. MacRobert	11.11.53
Ch. Colonsay Blacksmith	D	Ch. Raff of the Wells	Susan o' the Road	Miss Macfie	Mrs E. M. Smith	19.4.54
Ch. Cabaret Clementine	B	Ch. Cabaret Conservative	Phoebe Field	Miss Monkhouse	Miss Gaisford St Lawrence	5.7.54
Ch. Jellmont Justice	B	Ch. Lindally Briar	Caesar's Queen	Mrs Jellings	Mrs Jellings	17.2.54

202

	Sex	Sire	Dam		Owner	Date
1957						
Ch. Duxfordham Marvel	D	Duxfordham Dapper Dan of Dalmally	Aster of Widdington	Air Commodore Gore	Mrs Gore	20.6.55
Ch. Illyricum Independence	D	Postchaise Shadow	Rosa Canina of Illyricum	Mrs Aldrich-Blake	Mrs Aldrich-Blake	26.9.55
Ch. Tompkins of the Towpath	D	Ch. Dalwynn Diehard	Twinkle of the Towpath	Mrs P. Parker	Mrs Hill	28.2.56
Ch. Fanhill Fleur of Queenwood	B	Ch. Aldham George of Elberton	Nuffy Nydell	Mrs Woodyatt	Mrs Woodyatt	26.3.56
Ch. Gillian the Gangstress	B	Inglefield Rex	Gowan the Granger	J. W. Brown	J. W. Brown	29.8.54
Ch. Lazaars Gay Gipsy of Greenmount	B	Ch. Dalwynn Diehard	Ch. Lazaars Georgette	Dr and Mrs Piper	Mrs Caldwell	23.2.55
1958						
Ch. Duxfordham Neptune	D	Duxfordham Dapper Dan of Dalmally	Duxfordham Lady Luck	Air Commodore Gore	Air Commodore Gore	7.11.55
Ch. Tantivvey Illyricum Pyrus	D	Postchaise Shadow	Rima of Illyricum	Miss I. B. Clay	N. Cook	11.5.56
Ch. Greenmount Greensleeves	B	Ch. Tompkins of the Towpath	Ch. Lazaars Gay Gipsy of Greenmount	Dr and Mrs Piper	Dr and Mrs Piper	17.2.58
1959						
Ch. Howbeck Admiral	D	Ch. Duxfordham Marvel	Colonsay Salacia	Mrs P. M. Hay	Mrs P. M. Hay	8.11.57

Name	Sex	Sire	Dam	Owner	Breeder	Date of Birth
Ch. Postchaise Minstrel	D	Postchaise Shadow	Postchaise Kayenne	E. W. Davies	J. B. Richards	29.5.57
Ch. Shandy of Bonayr	D	Tawny of the Towpath	Golden Glint of Bonayr	Mrs B. E. Hoyle	T. Longworth	26.6.55
Ch. Tantivvey Brill	D	Ch. Tantivvey Illyricum Pyrus	Cobbinend Canter	Mrs G. B. Ellis	Miss I. B. Clay	18.7.57

1960

Name	Sex	Sire	Dam	Owner	Breeder	Date of Birth
Ch. Colonsay Dons Rapier	D	Ch. Tompkins of the Towpath	Colonsay Victory Morn	D. Stalker	Miss Macfie	16.3.58
Ch. Kurnool Echelon	D	Phaeland Cabaret Canopus	Kurnool Nutmeg	Mrs Macdonald Smith	Mrs A. Walford	29.9.57
Ch. Berricot Baroness Barbara	B	Duxfordham Dapper Dan of Dalmally	Colonsay Victory	Mrs Usher	Mrs Usher	3.2.58
Ch. Marshmallow of Widdington	B	Grapevine of Widdington	Violet of Widdington	Mrs M. S. Clegg	Mrs Hayman	19.1.58
Ch. Phaeland Lady Beauty	B	Phaeland Cabaret Canopus	Kurnool Quince	Mrs L. M. Gatheral	Mrs E. Wilson	27.11.55
Ch. Washakie Starlight	B	Ch. Duxfordham Marvel	Washakie Galaxy	Air Commodore Gore	Mrs McClellan	3.9.57

1961						
Ch. Colonsay Three Bells	D	Colonsay Bellbottom Joe	Fair Clippie	Miss Macfie	Mrs P. M. Lea	6.5.59
Ch. Creskeld Simba	D	Kurnool Rogue	Dinah of Middleham	Miss P. Dewhirst	Mrs N. Crump	24.4.57
Ch. Merithew Michael	D	Domino of Thornby	Brandy of Birch	Mr and Mrs R. H. Wertheim	Mr and Mrs R. H. Wertheim	28.1.58
Ch. Spenbrooke Saracen of Greenmount	D	Ch. Tompkins of the Towpath	Spenbrooke Satin Slippers	Dr and Mrs Piper	Mrs Stockman	7.6.57
Ch. Bellet Semmering Spot On	B	Tantivvey Blaze	Kingcup of Widdington	Mrs M. MacRobert	Mrs L. J. Allen	26.4.59
Ch. Tantivvey So'west Mystic	B	Ch. Tantivvey Illyricum Pyrus	Tantivvey Felicia	Miss I. B. Clay	J. Feast	15.9.59
1962						
Ch. Berricot Black Magic	D	Ch. Tantivvey Illyricum Pyrus	Berricot Belinda	Mrs Usher	Mrs Usher	18.5.59
Ch. Merithew Hey Presto	D	Ch. Tantivvey Illyricum Pyrus	Merithew Mandy	R. Finch	Mr and Mrs R. H. Wertheim	21.6.59
Ch. Phaeland Enterprise	D	Ch. Tweedle of the Towpath	Ch. Phaeland Lady Beauty	Mrs Gatheral	Mrs Gatheral	8.7.58
Ch. Widdington Oliver	D	Grapevine of Widdington	Landau Josephine	Mrs Jaques	Miss Oliver	17.4.58
Ch.Cabaret Cakewalk	B	Cabaret Carbon Copy	Cabaret Camria	Miss Monkhouse	Miss Monkhouse	26.10.62

Name	Sex	Sire	Dam	Owner	Breeder	Date of Birth
Ch. Illyricum Catriona Fraama	B	Ch. Illyricum Independence	Plume Poppy	Mrs Aldrich-Blake	Mrs J. S. Jones	14.3.60
Ch. Phaeland Illyricum Pandora	B	Ch. Illyricum Independence	Dawn of Dalbeattie	Mrs Gatheral	K. Jasper	16.2.59
1963						
Ch. Berricot Buccaneer	D	Ch. Colonsay Dons Rapier	Berricot Bryony	Mrs Kaufmann	Mrs Usher	16.4.59
Ch. Washakie Heirloom	D	Washakie Jubilee	Spenbrooke Sarong	Mrs McClellan	Mrs McClellan	23.4.61
Ch. Duxfordham Bronze Gleam	B	Duxfordham Dapper Dan of Dalmally	Sally of Saltash	Air Commodore Gore	Mrs Gale	20.3.61
Ch. Pompadally Pygmalion	B	Tantivvey George	Pompadally Gay Domino	Mrs S. A. Green	Mrs S. A. Green	15.6.60
Ch. Fulbeck Spanish Polka	B	Ch. Tompkins of the Towpath	Fulbeck Colrador	J. R. Tatham	J. R. Tatham	5.3.61
Ch. Greenmount Golden Guinea	B	Ch. Howbeck Admiral	Ch. Greenmount Greensleeves	Dr and Mrs Piper	Dr and Mrs Piper	2.3.62
Ch. Illyricum Mopsa	B	Ch. Illyricum Independence	Illyricum Tollgate Araminta	Mrs Aldrich-Blake	Mrs Aldrich-Blake	20.6.61
1964						
Ch. Colonsay April Jest	D	Colonsay Redhanded Simon	Colonsay Lady Ann	Miss Susan Gatherall	Mrs M. Marshall	1.4.62

Ch. Greenmount Grindewald	D	Colonsay Don's Rapier	Ch. Greenmount Greensleeves	Mrs G. Eady	Dr and Mrs Piper	1.2.61
Ch. Phaeland Maigret	D	Ch. Phaeland Enterprise	Kurnool Nutmeg	Miss Susan Gatherall	Mrs A. Walford	15.10.61
Ch. Horsemans Partner	B	Ch. Greenmount Grindewald	Horsemans Habit	Miss J. Agate	Miss J. Agate	2.3.63
Ch. Merithew Nannette of Istria	B	Domino of Thornby	Brandy of Birch	Mr C. Leutchford	Mr and Mrs Wertheim	4.4.61
Ch. Duxfordham Prince Tarquin	D	Ch. Duxfordham Neptune	Peryth Matilda	Air Commodore Gore	Mrs B. Turney	21.1.61

1965

Ch. Greenmount Greco of Istria	D	Ch. Howbeck Admiral	Ch. Greenmount Greensleeves	Mr Luetchford	Dr and Mrs Piper	2.3.62
Ch. Hot Brandy of Ascotheath	D	Ch. Howbeck Admiral	Grey Topper of Ascotheath	Mr and Mrs D. Cudd	Mr and Mrs D. Cudd	7.11.63
Ch. Postchaise Monarch	D	Ch. Postchaise Minstrel	Pixie of Green Alders	Mr E. Davies	Mrs M. Willson	27.1.63
Ch. Berricot Blonde Bombshell	B	Ch. Berricot Black Magic	Colonsay Sunbeam	Mrs B. Usher	Mrs B. Usher	15.3.64
Ch. Ivelda Iris	B	Ch. Spenbrook Saracen of Greenmount	Greenmount Gazelle	Mrs J. Gardner	Mr. I. Taylor	27.9.62

Name	Sex	Sire	Dam	Owner	Breeder	Date of Birth
1966						
Ch. Fanhill Faune	B	Ch. Colonsay April Jest	Ch. Fanhill Fleur of Queenwood	Mrs Woodyatt	Mrs Woodyatt	16.5.64
Ch. Greenmount Grace Darling	B	Ch. Tompkins of the Towpath	Ch. Greenmount Golden Guinea	Dr and Mrs Piper	Dr and Mrs Piper	24.2.65
Ch. Greenmount Grenville of Starmead	D	Ch. Duxfordham Marvel	Ch. Greenmount Greensleeves	Mr and Mrs Wholey	Dr and Mrs Piper	7.4.63
Ch. Hansom Leprechaun	B	Ch. Merithew Hey Presto	Beauty's Glow	Mr and Mrs Finch	J. Carney	2.5.64
Ch. Duxfordham Magic Orb	D	Ch. Duxfordham Marvel	Sookie Soughbread	Air Commodore Gore	Miss Oliver	23.2.63
Ch. Coachbarn Classic	D	Ch. Greenmount Grenville of Starmead	Coachbarn Spots of News	Mrs M. Chapman	Mrs M. Chapman	17.10.64
Ch. Son of Alexander	D	Alexander of Ascotheath	Duxfordham Crystal	Mrs F. Powell	Mr Trenhaill	18.7.64
1967						
Ch. Olbero O'Rourke	D	Fanhill Fillip	Odette of Olbero	Mr and Mrs Curtis	Mr and Mrs Rance	17.3.64
Ch. Gentleman of Erin	D	Farnforest Timothy	Merithew Sheba	Mr J. Locke	F. W. Granger	2.7.63
Ch. Cabaret Crown Derby	B	Cabaret Checkpoint Charlie	Beautache Black Spangle	Miss Monkhouse	Mr D. Wild	2.5.64

Ch. Duxfordham Magic Empire	D	Duxfordham Empire Jamboree	Duxfordham Nicolette	Air Commodore Gore	Miss M. East	9.7.65
Ch. Cabaret Cruacham	B	Cabaret Checkpoint Charlie	Kingsowne Wanda	Miss Monkhouse	Mr J. King	5.10.64
Ch. Pamphard Cabaret Ceramica	B	Cabaret Charaline	Capriole Dilly's Daughter	Mrs P. Marshall	Mr A. Neville	5.3.65

1968

Ch. Dalpanda Deb's Delight	D	Oudenard Rustic	Nuna of Widdington	Mrs Diana Hamilton	Mrs Clegg	28.3.63
Ch. Clydevale Don Camillo	D	Clydevale Ace	Clydevale Cleopatra	Mrs C. Wharton	Mrs C. Wharton	4.10.64
Ch. Olbero O'Keefe	D	Fanhill Fillip	Tessa of the Chaise	Mr and Mrs P. Rance	Mr and Mrs P. Rance	17.3.64
Ch. Delvallie Brougham Bright Boy	D	Howbeck Admiral	Ch. Ivelda Iris	Mrs B. Le Chanu	Mrs Gardner	27.4.66
Ch. Illyricum Camelina	B	Postchaise Monarch	Ch. Illyricum Mopsa	Mrs E. Aldrich-Blake	Mrs E. Aldrich-Blake	3.5.65
Ch. Olbero Orabella	B	Ch. Olbero O'Keefe	Tessette of Camelot	Mrs Rance	Mr and Mrs Santer	15.7.66
Ch. Chica of Lodgehill	B	Ch. Greenmount Grindelwald	Sabina of Lodgehill	Mrs Hill	Mrs Hill	14.3.65

Name	Sex	Sire	Dam	Owner	Breeder	Date of Birth
Ch. Clydevale Timmy Trew	D	Ch. Clydevale Don Camillo	Isola Bella	Miss C. S. Smith	Mr and Mrs Sutton	14.2.66
Ch. Roadster Rolando	D	Fanhill Fabian	Roadster Dimity	Messrs B. E. and D. J. Conway	Mr and Mrs Playford	7.5.66
1969						
Ch. Appaloosa Starquest	B	Appaloosa Harlequin	Appaloosa Stardom	Miss A. S. Bale	Mrs E. Felton	24.3.66
Ch. Delvallie Blueprint	D	Ch. Delvallie Brougham Bright Boy	Delvallie Silver-pine Symphony	Mrs B. G. Le Chanu	Mrs B. G. Le Chanu	22.12.67
Ch. Horsemans Vogue	B	Fanhill Fabian	Ch. Horsemans Partner	Miss Agate	Miss Agate	23.4.67
Ch. Illyricum Moreton Aurelia	B	Ch. Son of Alexander	Illyricum Clary	Mrs E. Aldrich-Blake	Mrs V. Nye	23.5.67
Ch. Northpleck Lady Warwick	B	Northpleck Watney Man	Spartan Dolly	Mr A. G. North	Mrs B. Ingram	17.5.67
Ch. Spott On Henry of Bransbegin	D	Ch. Hot Brandy of Ascotheath	Roslyn of Ascotheath	Mrs J. Willison	Mr and Mrs J.B.C. Evans	20.4.67
Ch. Silvanwood Golden Sovereign	B	Cabaret Check-point Charlie	Silvanwood Amanda	Miss I. B. Clay	Mesdames E. M. Wood and W. D. Bargate	7.5.66
Ch. Stallions Sampson	D	Ch. Colonsay April Jest	Stallions Colonsay Noontide	Mrs H. Godfrey	Mrs H. Godfrey	10.3.67

210

Name	Sex	Sire	Dam	Breeder	Owner	Date
Ch. Titan of Chacombe	D	Withalder Warlord	Tantivvey Rowena	Mrs M. K. Greening	Mrs D. Cameron	27.5.66

1970

Name	Sex	Sire	Dam	Breeder	Owner	Date
Ch. Brockhampton Baronet	D	Ch. Greenmount Grenville of Starmead	Fanhill Fay	Mr and Mrs F.G.A. Thompson	Mr and Mrs F.G.A. Thompson	31.5.67
Ch. Cabaret Cashleen	B	Cabaret Charlayne	Withalder Wardancer	Miss R. C. Monkhouse	Miss R. C. Monkhouse	23.2.68
Ch. Duxfordham Corraith Cosmonaut	D	Ch. Duxfordham Magic Empire	Duxford Grecian of Corraith	Air Commodore C. W. Gore	Mr J. Stout	8.2.68
Ch. Exhurst Etoile of Sydon	B	Ch. Olbero O'Rourke	Greenmount Gorgeous Gussie of Exhurst	Mr and Mrs D. Curtis	Mr F. Willey and Lady Astor	7.2.67
Ch. Konavije Miss Gorgeous	B	Ch. Colonsay April Jest	Greenmount Golden Glow	Miss S. Gatheral	Mrs M. M. Davidson	28.6.67
Ch. Marzelina Clausentum Dook	D	Ch. Washakie Heirloom	Wolfox's Clausentum Daphne	Mr and Mrs L. M. Cutts	Mrs H. A. and Miss J. M. Lanning	8.4.67
Ch. Phaeland Pompadally Persephone	B	Pompadally Illyricum Corin	Ch. Pompadally Pygmalion	Miss S. D. Gatheral	Major and Mrs S. Green	1.9.66
Ch. Tantivvey Fanhill Filomel	B	Fanhill Fabian	Ch. Fanhill Faune	Miss I. B. Clay	Mrs E. J. Woodyatt	26.4.68
Ch. Washakie Moonraker	D	Ch. Greenmount Grindelwald	Washakie Tantivvey Fidra	Mrs M. L. Tout	Mrs B. McCellan	20.1.66

Name	Sex	Sire	Dam	Owner	Breeder	Date of Birth
Ch. Washakie Othello	D	Ch. Washakie Moonraker	Washakie Clausentun Lucy	Mrs B. McClellan	Mrs B. McClellan	25.1.69
1971						
Ch. Brougham Babycham	B	Ch. Colonsay April Jest	Ch. Ivelda Iris	Mr and Mrs E. W. Gardner	Mr and Mrs E. W. Gardner	15.10.67
Ch. Delvallie Gay Girl	B	Ch. Delvallie Brougham Bright Boy	Delvallie Silverpine Symphony	Mrs B. Le Chanu	Mrs B. Le Chanu	29.7.69
Ch. Lodgehill Masterpiece	D	Ch. Tompkins of the Towpath	Ch. Chica of Lodge Hill	Mrs V. Hill	Mrs V. Hill	9.4.66
Ch. Midnight Runway of Pentwyn	D	Midnight Storm of Pentwyn	Dawn of Pentwyn	Mrs R. V. Stock	Mrs R. V. Stock	4.1.70
Ch. Phaeland Patron	D	Phaeland Lucas	Phaeland Fanlight	Miss S. Gatheral	Mrs Yates-Moor	29.7.67
1972						
Ch. Delvallie Bright Spot	B	Ch. Delvallie Brougham Bright Boy	Delvallie Lady Go Lightly	Mrs E. Craig	Mrs B. Le Chanu	29.10.67
Ch. Greenmount Gemini	B	Marcus Antonious of Rhodes	Greenmount Gaerwendry	Mrs B. Smith	Mrs C. Mackenzie	19.4.65
Ch. Highstables Twilight	B	Ch. Colonsay April Jest	Phaeland Simone Maigret	Mrs E. Paterson	Mr and Mrs I. Peplow	7.2.69
Ch. Iceni Boudica	B	Ch. Colonsay April Jest	Phaeland Fenella	Mrs S. Crosby	Mrs E. Sharpe	3.3.66

Name	Sex	Sire	Dam	Breeder	Owner	Date
Ch. Stallions Oscar	D	Ch. Delvallie Blueprint	Stallions Wood Nymph	Mrs H. Godfrey	S. Petchey	2.3.70
Ch. Wagonette Piber Royal Lancer	D	Brougham Banker	Alandors Silver Gem	Mr and Mrs L. Budge	Mr and Mrs P. Collins	28.1.70
Ch. Trumpeters Laureola	B	Washakie Blackwatch	Trumpeters Tansy	Mrs S. Michael	Mrs Mackinlay	4.4.70
Ch. Appaloosa Stardante	D	Appaloosa Sunspinner	Ch. Appaloosa Starquest	Mr J. Gretton	Miss A. G. Bale	7.1.70
1973						
Ch. Washakie Margaret	B	Ch. Washakie Moonraker	Washakie Clausentum Lucy	Mrs P. Kindersly	Mrs McClellan	1.8.71
Ch. Leagarth Northern Escort	D	Colonsay Sir Thomas Modyford	Leagarth Magnetic Sand	Mr J. S. Hally	Mr J. S. Hally	28.9.70
Ch. Trumpeters Hotspur	D	Ch. Delvallie Blue Print	Colonsay Sea Coral	Mrs M. Kaufmann	Mrs M. Kaufmann	4.6.69
Ch. Delvallie Highland Wedding	D	Ch. Delvallie Brougham Bright Boy	Delvallie Silverpine Sympathy	Mrs Le Chanu	Mrs Le Chanu	3.12.71
Ch. Glenbrook Annabelle of Ascotheath	B	Ch. Clydevale Timmy Trew	Gay Whisper of Ascotheath	Mr and Mrs D. Cudd	Mrs Giddings	11.5.69
Ch. Olbero Onceuponatime	B	Brougham Banker	Renhill April Dancer	Mr and Mrs P. M. Rance	R. Sharp and N. Warner	3.5.71

Name	Sex	Sire	Dam	Owner	Breeder	Date of Birth
Ch. Sophia of Randan	B	Ch. Gentleman of Erin	Meriel Marianna Imogen	Misses Longmuir and Scatchard	Misses Longmuir and Scatchard	26.2.68
Ch. Fanhill Fabulous Lady of Ravenswing	B	Brougham Banker	Ch. Fanhill Faune	Mr and Mrs W. S. Marshall	Mrs J. Woodyatt	14.12.71
Ch. Tollcross Fanhill Faraoh	D	Brougham Banker	Ch. Fanhill Faune	Mrs M. K. Greening	Mrs J. Woodyatt	14.12.71
Ch. Hansom Hilarity	B	Ch. Colonsay April Jest	Ch. Hansom Leprechaun	Mr and Mrs W. McKay	Mr and Mrs Finch	28.1.70
1974 Ch. Olbero Overthemoon	D	Ch. Wagonette Piber Royal Lancer	Ch. Olbero Orabella	Mr and Mrs C. Foster	Mr and Mrs P. M. Rance	21.5.72
Ch. Tirriemore Twilight	B	Brougham Banker	Tullah of Essex	Mrs F. Child	Mrs F. Child	13.11.70
Ch. Weaponess Sweetalk Sophie	B	Ch. Phaeland Patron	Geronimo Bellbird	Mrs M. Pilgrim	Miss J. Haynes	18.9.71
Ch. Oudenarde Golden May	B	Ch. Delvallie Blueprint	Oudenarde Brown Honey	Mrs D. Hamilton and Mrs G. Oldham	Mrs D. and Miss H. Hamilton	12.2.70
Ch. Starmead Sirius	D	Ch. Berricot Black Magic	Starmead Saturn	Mr and Mrs J. Wholey	Mr and Mrs J. Wholey	26.10.68

Name	Sex	Sire	Dam	Breeder	Owner	Date
Ch. Olbero Overtherainbow	B	Ch. Wagonette Piber Royal Lancer	Ch. Olbero Orabella	Mr and Mrs P. M. Rance	Mr and Mrs P. M. Rance	21.5.72
Ch. Phaeland Phreda	B	Ch. Phaeland Patron	Lady Sasha	Miss S. Gatheral	Mrs Kirton	4.11.71
Ch. Phaeland Phisherman	D	Ch. Phaeland Patron	Illyricum Clary	Miss S. Gatheral	Miss S. Gatheral	17.10.72
Ch. Randan Emporium	D	Ch. Clydevale Don Camillo	Randan Ermine	Misses Longmuir and Scatchard	Misses Longmuir and Scatchard	31.8.73

CHAMPIONS SINCE 1974

Name	Sex	Sire	Dam	Breeder	Owner	Date
Ch. Dandale Tudor Rose	B	Ch. Tollcross Fanhill Faraoh	Dame Paulet of Henhurst	Mr and Mrs C. T. Dandy	Mr and Mrs C. T. Dandy	8.2.73
Ch. Pampard Plum Pud'n	D	Ch. Washakie Othello	Ch. Pampard Cabaret Ceramica	Mrs P. Marshall	Mrs P. Marshall	26.10.72
Ch. Coachbarn Cinnamon	B	Greenmount Gobbi	Coachbarn Carlotta	Mrs M. Chapman	Mrs M. Chapman	13.3.73
Ch. Manxhaven Grenadier of Greenmount	D	Greenmount Goblin	Greenmount Grandiflora	Mr and Mrs K. Hobson	Mr B. M. H. Kinrade	13.3.71
Ch. Cabaret Cashmere	B	Cabaret Cashaway	Cabaret Cupacoco	Mrs R. Monkhouse	Mrs R. Monkhouse	13.8.73

Name	Sex	Sire	Dam	Owner	Breeder	Date of Birth
Ch. Pampard Pollywolly Doodle	B	Brougham Banker	Pampard Pete	Mrs J. Shaw	Mrs P. Marshall	8.2.72
Ch. Northern Grenada of Leagarth	D	Ch. Leagarth Northern Escort	Gramont Gila of Canusaig	Mr J. S. Hally	Mrs M. E. Dempster	7.3.73
Ch. Starmead Sky at Night	D	Ch. Starmead Sirius	Starmead Serene Sun	Mr and Mrs J. Wholey	Mr and Mrs J. Wholey	3.1.70
Ch. Northpleck Softly Softly	D	Northpleck Hayride	Glenbrook Zuleika	Mrs P. North	Mr Barnes	7.4.74
Ch. Dallyvista Drummer Boy	D	Greenmount Grand Marnier	Ch. Greenmount Gemini	Mrs K. Hoskins	Mrs B. Smith	21.12.70
Ch. Horsemans Relay	B	Brougham Banker	Horsemans Good Intent	Mrs J. Agate-Hilton	Mrs J. Agate-Hilton	1.10.74
Ch. Greenmount Grebe	B	Ch. Washakie Othello	Ch. Greenmount Grace Darling	Mrs M. Chapman	Mrs P. Piper	18.10.72
Ch. Phaeland Phorgetmenot	B	Phaeland Jeeves	Washakie Wisteria	Miss M. Gatheral	Mrs J. Rigby	13.7.69
Ch. Gay Cavalier at Spotarton	D	Sceptre Snoopy	Rubaiyat Lucy Locket	Mrs G. Gregory	B. W. Clayton	17.7.71
Ch. Ascotheath Regency Belle	B	Ch. Hot Brandy of Ascotheath	Alexander's Girl	Mr and Mrs R. Hamilton	Mrs M. Malcolm	4.12.71
Ch. Bawhinnan Rpssdhu	D	Ch. Phaeland Patron	Ravold Missidentity	Mr and Mrs J. Whyte	Mr and Mrs J. Whyte	26.7.72

216

Name	Sex	Sire	Dam	Owner	Breeder	Date
Ch. Buffrey Savannah	B	Buffrey Effendi	Northpleck Obie Sue	Mr and Mrs J. Neath	Mr and Mrs B. Morton	25.5.74
Ch. Peroca Playboy	D	Ch. Delvallie Bright Boy	Tirriemore Trianco	Mr and Mrs D. Cresswell	Mr and Mrs D. Cresswell	12.5.72
Ch. Phaeland Phrederick	D	Ch. Colonsay April Jest	Tantivvey Middlefield Margo	Mr and Mrs W. McKay	Miss S. D. A. Gatheral	2.8.69
Ch. Appaloosa Sporting Chance	D	Ch. Charioteer Daniel	Appaloosa Gold Finger	Mrs A. Bale Stock	Mrs A. Bale Stock	9.1.75
Ch. Washakie Spotlight	D	Ch. Washakie Othello	Ch. Tirriemore Twilight	Mrs B. McClellan	Mrs F. Child	17.4.75
Ch. Delvallie Dark Bronze	D	Brougham Banker	Int. Ch. Delvallie Gay Girl	Miss S. D. A. Gatheral	Mr Le Chanu	5.9.73
Ch. Dalstead D'Artagnan	D	Ch. Washakie Othello	Dalstead Bronze Medallion	Mr and Mrs R. Steadman	Mr and Mrs R. Steadman	16.5.74
Ch. Dallux Dapple Damsel	B	Greenmount Grand Marnier	Duxfordham Intruder	Mr and Mrs C.M.P. Luxton	Mr and Mrs C.M.P. Luxton	27.11.72
Ch. Highstables Countess of Konavlje	B	Ch. Delvallie Dark Bronze	Camargue Charisma of Highstables	Mrs M. Davidson	C. Pedlow	18.5.75
Ch. Pickled Walnut from Pampard	B	Ch. Pampard Plum Pud'n	Travier Anglo Arab	Mrs P. Marshall	Mrs Brooking	22.4.76
Int. Ch. Clyedale Mastermind	D	Ch. Randan Emporium	Honeybee of Stirlingclose	Mrs P. Easton	Mrs C. T. Wharton	15.11.75

Name	Sex	Sire	Dam	Owner	Breeder	Date of Birth
Ch. Dalmark Pongo the Conqueror	D	Ch. Dallyvista Drummer Boy	Jewells Prima of Dalmark	Miss M. Kembrey	Miss M. Kembrey	26.2.75
Ch. Sceptre Snoopy	D	Ch. Titan of Chacombe	Sceptre Queen	Mr and Mrs B. Gregory	Mr and Mrs B. Gregory	17.5.69
Ch. Charioteer Daniel	D	Ch. Washakie Othello	Charioteer Calypso	Mrs J. Beale	Mrs Edwards	3.6.72
Ch. Weaponess Statesman of Pentwyn	D	Ch. Midnight Runaway of Pentwyn	Ch. Weaponess Sweetalk Sophie	Mrs B. Ball	Mrs P. Pilgrim	12.7.75
Ch. Randan Gaffer	D	Ch. Randan Emporium	Randan Firefly	Misses J. A. H. Longmuir and M. Scatchard	Misses J. A. H. Longmuir and M. Scatchard	14.3.76
Ch. Tantivvey Hester	B	Brougham Banker	Ch. Tantivvey Fanhill Filomel	Mrs S. Aldenhoven	Miss I. B. Clay	8.5.71
Ch. Phaeland Phrench Phern	B	Ch. Delvallie Blue Print	Phaeland Phern	Miss S. D. A. Gatheral	Miss S. D. A. Gatheral	23.7.75
Ch. Dhulea Demerara	B	Ch. Charioteer Daniel	Northpleck Lystra	Mr and Mrs S. Beaumont	Mrs S. P. Booth	5.2.74
Ch. Kerry Piper of Bosville	B	Brougham Banker	Highstables Petronella	Lady MacDonald of Sleat	Mr and Mrs Fitton	14.2.75
Ch. Suskarden Lady	B	Stallions Oscar	Francesca of Kenstaff	Mr F. Finch	Mr F. Finch	26.10.75

218

Ch. Dalregis Sugarplum Fairy	B		Sally of Newton Regis	Mrs P. M. Wilson	Mrs P. M. Wilson	5.3.75
Ch. Mattoria Apple of my Eye	B		Clydevale Julep	Mrs K. Brand	Mrs K. Brand	17.9.75
Ch. Knightstone Matilda	B	Washakie Illyricum Blue Magic	Ch. Washakie Margaret	Mrs L. Brown	Mrs P. Kindersley	1.8.74
Ch. Buffrey Jobee	D		Ch. Buffrey Savannah	Mr and Mrs J. Neath	Mr and Mrs J. Neath	1.4.77
Ch. Ravold Andy Capp	D	Ch. Delvallie Blue Print	Ravold Alice	Mr N. A. Graham	Mr N. A. Graham	10.2.77
Ch. Clausentum Red Arrow of Delvallie	D	Lippen Sands Ablaze	Clausentum Dot	Mr J. Le Chanu	Miss J. M. Lanning	25.9.76
Ch. Lyndora Golden Wedding	D	Ch. Delvallie Highland Wedding	Lyndora Gold Kelly	Mr B. E. Williams	Mrs D. Bury	26.8.76
Ch. Bright Amber at Spotarton	D	Ch. Sceptre Snoopy	Rubaiyat Lucy Locket	Mr and Mrs B. Gregory	B. W. Clayton	17.7.71
Ch. Teisanlap Hermione of Trumpeters	B	Wittenham Winters Tale	Welsh Poppy of Teisanlap	Mrs M. Kaufman	Mr and Mrs S. Beaumont	4.3.76
Ch. Pride of the Stallions	B	Ch. Stallions Oscar	Lady Penelope Pique	Mrs H. Godfrey	J. Clacey	20.3.72
Ch. Farrowsmiths Miss Mischief	B	Ch. Gay Cavalier of Spotarton	Farrowsmiths Dainty Miss	Mr W. A. Smith	Mr W. A. Smith	5.10.77

Name	Sex	Sire	Dam	Owner	Breeder	Date of Birth
Ch. Charioteer Fulmar	D	Charioteer Cetos	Shuna Osprey	Mrs W. M. Edwards	Mrs W. M. Edwards	17.9.76
Ch. Lizadal Lancers Lad	D	Ch. Wagonette Piber Royal Lancer	Tovilstone Turkish Delight	Miss E. A. Adams	Miss E. A. Adams	14.6.76
Ch. Merrybriar Ludwig	D	Ch. Charioteer Daniel	Gilpenny Lorna Doone Star	Mrs W. A. Jenkins	Mrs W. A. Jenkins	18.4.77
Ch. Pasea Pegasus	D	Ch. Delvallie Dark Bronze	Pasea Sparton Personality	Mr D. C. Blaxall	Mr D. C. Blaxall	22.2.76
Ch. Whealgrace Wamura Wiggy	D	Craigshill Magnus	Tighna Bruinch	Mr and Mrs D. Ross	Mr and Mrs D. Ross	18.2.76
Ch. Dalmark the Daydreamer from Dallyvista	B	Ch. Dallyvista Drummer Boy	Jewells Prima at Dalmark	Mr and Mrs M. Smith	Miss M. Kembrey	22.8.76
Ch. Olbero Operasinger	B	Ch. Wagonette Piber Royal Lancer	Ch. Olbero Orabella	Mr and Mrs J. Zoutos	Mr and Mrs P. Rance	25.3.74
Ch. Illyricum Bettrys	B	Illyricum Targe	Illyricum Knightstone Fortune Teller	Mrs J. E. Preen	Mrs E. Aldrich-Blake	7.9.75
Ch. Tamaron Tic Tac of Bawhinnan	B	Int. Ch. Clydevale Mastermind	Trumpeters Honeysuckle Rose	Mr and Mrs J. C. Whyte	Mr N. Smith	1.9.78

220

Name	Sex	Sire	Dam	Breeder	Owner	Date
Ch. Illyricum Isa of Farforest	B	Cabaret Cashaway	Farforest Crusty	Mrs E. Aldrich-Blake	Mrs B. Daniel	2.10.76
Ch. Miragua Pendragon	D	Ch. Delvallie Dark Bronze	Miragua Juniper	Mrs F.C.T. Hartley	Mrs F.C.T. Hartley	2.8.76
Ch. Fallowfield Firelight	D	Ch. Phaeland Phiddlesticks	Luscious Lass of Fallowfield	Mrs C. Lewis	Mrs C. Lewis	21.2.79
Ch. Fallowfield Firedancer	B	Ch. Phaeland Phiddlesticks	Luscious Lass of Fallowfield	Mrs C. Lewis	Mrs C. Lewis	11.7.77
Ch. Tamaron Twilight Gold of Trumpeters	B	Int. Ch. Clydevale Mastermind	Trumpeters Honeysuckle Rose	Mrs M. Kaufman	Mr N. A. Smith	11.9.78
Ch. Psychic Power at Pampard	D	Washakie Illyricum Blue Magic	Clairvoyant of Panas	Mrs P. Marshall	Mr I. G. Marshall	22.7.79
Ch. Hartspring Hillbilly	D	Olbero Olafsson	Moortrekker Maid Marian	Mr and Mrs B. Taylor	Mr and Mrs B. Taylor	19.5.77
Ch. Tantivvey Target of Olbero	D	Fanhill Fred	Old Gold of Tantivvey	Mr and Mrs P. Rance	Miss I. B. Clay	3.1.77
Ch. Olbero Organised Confusion	D	Ch. Tantivvey Target of Olbero	Ch. Olbero Overtherainbow	Mr and Mrs P. Rance	Mr and Mrs. P. Rance	1.11.78
Ch. Beaurydown Bray of Furzedale	B	Ch. Charioteer Daniel	Knightstone Marilla	Mrs J. Beale	Mr and Mrs Palmer	30.12.78
Ch. Wardell Whatsizname	D	Ch. Lizadal Lancers Lad	Gaypals Miss Milly	Mr S. Lerner	Mrs Archer	21.2.80

221

Name	Sex	Sire	Dam	Owner	Breeder	Date of Birth
Ch. Weaponess Cragvallie Curry	B	Ch. Delvallie Dark Bronze	Weaponess Sweetalk Sophie	Mrs I. Gardner	Mrs P. Pilgrim	18.12.77
Ch. Milldance Bossonova	D	Ch. Dalmark Pongo the Conqueror	Casilla Camille	Mrs S. Miller	Mrs S. Miller	20.10.78
Ch. Washakie Bellajo of Buffrey	B	Ch. Buffrey Jobee	Washakie Marbella	Mr and Mrs J. Neath	Mrs B. McClellan	26.2.80
Ch. Olbero Onsdag Moln of Theakston	B	Ch. Tantivvey Targer of Olbero	Olbero Onsdag	Mrs J. Atkinson	Mr and Mrs P. Rance	28.4.79
Ch. Washakie Winona	B	Ch. Buffrey Jobee	Washakie Marbella	Mr and Mrs P. A. Stannard	Mrs B. McClellan	26.2.80
Ch. Phaeland Phiddlesticks	D	Delvallie Dark Bronze	Ascotheath Regency Belle	Miss S. D. A. Gatheral	Mrs M. Hamilton	28.1.78
Ch. Ravold Arabella	B	Ch. Phaeland Phiddlesticks	Ravold Alice	Mr N. Graham	Mr N. Graham	20.10.79
Ch. Phaeland Phishpie	B	Ch. Phaeland Phiddlesticks	Phaeland Phishphinger	Miss S. D. A. Gatheral	Miss S. D. A. Gatheral	4.7.80
Ch. Tollcross Tinsmith	D	Ch. Delvallie Dark Bronze	Tollcross Temptation	Mrs M. Greening	Mrs M. Greening	9.4.80
Ch. Washakie Debonair	D	Ch. Buffrey Jobee	Washakie Tanya	Mrs McClellan and Miss Goff	Mrs P. Kindersley	20.7.81

Name	Sex	Sire	Dam	Breeder	Owner	Date
Ch.Konavlje Miss Fabulous	B	Ch. Charioteer Daniel	Ch. Highstables Countess of Konavlje	Mrs M. Davidson	Mrs M. Davidson	14.7.80
Ch. Tantivvey Tawney Owl of Olbero	D	Ch. Hartspring Hillbilly	Tantivvey Thelma	Mr and Mrs P. Rance	Miss I. B. Clay	4.12.81
Ch. Sanfelipe Shicago	D	Sanfelipe Shaun	Sanfelipe Smyla	Mr and Mrs W. McKay	Mr and Mrs W. McKay	10.2.78
Ch. Dalmark Ellie the Showgirl	B	Ch. Miragua Pendragon	Pennicol Currant Bun at Dalmark	Mrs L. Butler	Miss M. Kembrey	19.3.81
Ch. Cragvallie Caprice	B	Ch. Olbero Organised Confusion	Cragvallie Coriander	Mrs I. Gardner	Mrs I. Gardner	8.12.81
Ch. Dapple Dana of Sidlaw	B	Sidlaw Dapper Dandy	Nutmeg Sargor	Mrs Steen	Mr and Mrs D. J. Wilson	6.1.80
Ch. Brythennek Bellona	B	Ch. Psychic Power at Pampard	Ch. Washakie Winona	Mr and Mrs M. Fisher	Mr and Mrs P. Stannard	11.4.82
Ch. Spring Classic of Appaloosa	D	Sebastian D'Canter of Appaloosa	Penelope Llewpartog	Mrs A. Bale-Stock	Mr and Mrs F. Dent	7.8.82
Ch. Brythennek Basil Fawlty	D	Ch. Psychic Power at Pampard	Ch. Washakie Winona	Mr and Mrs J. Watson	Mr and Mrs P. Stannard	11.4.82
Ch. Dhulea Daffy Down Dilly	B	Ch. Randan Gaffer	Dhulea Damosel	Mrs. S. P. Booth	Mrs S. P. Booth	4.8.78
Ch. Disneytime at Spotarton	B	Startime at Spotarton	Lady Pinter	Miss C. J. Gregory	B. J. Bowers	16.8.81

Name	Sex	Sire	Dam	Owner	Breeder	Date of Birth
Ch. Olbero Organdie Collar	B	Ch. Wardell Whatsizname	Organdie of Olbero	Mr and Mrs P. Rance	Mr and Mrs P. Rance	16.3.82
Ch. Aconitum Caesar of Marverte	D	Ch. Charioteer Daniel	Aconitum of Church Farm	Mrs M. Green	Mrs J. Diment	21.5.77

BIBLIOGRAPHY

Ash, Edward C. *Dogs, their History and Development*, Benn (1927).
The New Book of the Dog, Cassell (1938).
Auerbach, Charlotte. *The Science of Genetics*, Hutchinson (1962).
Bell, Thomas. *History of British Quadrupeds* (1837).
Berners, Dame Juliana. *The Boke of St Albans* (1480).
Bewick, Thomas. *History of Quadrupeds* (1791).
British Dalmatian Club Handbooks (1934–63).
Buffon, Count de. *Natural History* (1772).
Burns, Marca and Fraser, M. N. *Genetics of the Dog*, second edition, Oliver & Boyd (1966).
Caius, Dr John. *De Canis Britannicus Libellus* (1560).
Croxton-Smith, A. *About Our Dogs*, Ward, Lock and Co. (1931).
Dogs since 1900, Andrew Dakers (1950).
Drury, W. D. *British Dogs*, L. Upcott Gill (1903).
Fleming, Abraham. *Of English Dogs* (1660).
Frankling, Eleanor. *Practical Dog Breeding and Genetics*, Popular Dogs (1961).
Gesner, Conrad. *Historiae Animalium* (1587).
Gore, Catherine. *Dalmatians*, W. and G. Foyle Ltd (1962).
Hubbard, Clifford L. B. *The Dalmatian Handbook*, Nicholson and Watson (1957).
Kalmus, H., and Crump, Lettice. *Genetics*, Pelican Books Ltd (1948).
Lauer, H. Fred. *The Dalmatian*, S. W. Groome Ltd, U.S.A. (1907).
Little, Clarence C., SC.D. *The Inheritance of Coat Colour in Dogs*, Cornell University Press (1957).
Pearce, the Rev. Thomas (Idstone). *The Dog*, 3rd edition (1872).
Saunders, James. *The Dalmatian and All about it*, Dog World (1932).
Shaw, Vero. *The Illustrated Book of the Dog*, Cassell Petter & Co. Galpin (1882).
Smith, Dodie. *One Hundred and One Dalmatians*, Heinemann (1956).

225

Smith, Col. Hamilton. *Naturalists' Library Vol. 10*, Mammalia (1840).

Taplin, W. *The Sportsman's Cabinet* (1803).

Topsell, Edward. *The Historie of Fourfooted Beastes* (1607).

Walsh, J. H. (Stonehenge). *The Dog*, Longmans Green and Dyer (1867).
  Dogs of the British Islands, 2nd and 5th editions, The Field (1872 and 1886).

Whitney, Leon. *How to breed Dogs*, Orange Judd Publishing Co. (1957).

Youatt, William. *The Dog*, Green and Dyer (1854).

INDEX

In the following index, 'Dalmatian' is abbreviated to 'D'.